Fair Trade

Other Books in the Current Controversies Series

Fair Trade

Debra A. Miller, Book Editor

GREENHAVEN PRESS
A part of Gale, Cengage Learning

GALE
CENGAGE Learning™

Detroit • New York • San Francisco • New Haven, Conn • Waterville, Maine • London

Christine Nasso, *Publisher*
Elizabeth Des Chenes, *Managing Editor*

© 2010 Greenhaven Press, a part of Gale, Cengage Learning

Gale and Greenhaven Press are registered trademarks used herein under license.

For more information, contact:
Greenhaven Press
27500 Drake Rd.
Farmington Hills, MI 48331-3535
Or you can visit our Internet site at gale.cengage.com

For product information and technology assistance, contact us at

Gale Customer Support, 1-800-877-4253
For permission to use material from this text or product, submit all requests online at www.cengage.com/permissions

Further permissions questions can be emailed to permissionrequest@cengage.com

Articles in Greenhaven Press anthologies are often edited for length to meet page requirements. In addition, original titles of these works are changed to clearly present the main thesis and to explicitly indicate the author's opinion. Every effort is made to ensure that Greenhaven Press accurately reflects the original intent of the authors. Every effort has been made to trace the owners of copyrighted material.

Cover image © Andrew Fox/Terra/Corbis.

LIBRARY OF CONGRESS CATALOGING-IN-PUBLICATION DATA

Fair trade / Debra A. Miller, Book Editor.
    p. cm. -- (Current controversies)
    Includes bibliographical references and index.
    ISBN 978-0-7377-4703-4 (hardcover) -- ISBN 978-0-7377-4704-1 (pbk.)
    1. International trade--Juvenile literature. 2. Competition, Unfair--Juvenile literature. I. Miller, Debra A.
    HF1379.F337 2010
    382'.3--dc22
                                       2009039165

Printed in the United States of America
2 3 4 5 6 7 13 12 11 10

Contents

Chapter 1: Is Fair Trade a Beneficial Policy?

Yes, Fair Trade Is a Beneficial Policy.

Chapter 2: Should Fair Trade Be Extended to Large Companies?

Chapter 3: Is Fair Trade Compatible with Free Trade?

Yes, Fair Trade Is Compatible with Free Trade.

Chapter 4: How Can the Fair Trade System Be Improved?

Foreword

By definition, controversies are "discussions of questions in which opposing opinions clash" (*Webster's Twentieth Century Dictionary Unabridged*). Few would deny that controversies are a pervasive part of the human condition and exist on virtually every level of human enterprise. Controversies transpire between individuals and among groups, within nations and between nations. Controversies supply the grist necessary for progress by providing challenges and challengers to the status quo. They also create atmospheres where strife and warfare can flourish. A world without controversies would be a peaceful world; but it also would be, by and large, static and prosaic.

The Series' Purpose

The purpose of the *Current Controversies* series is to explore many of the social, political, and economic controversies dominating the national and international scenes today. Titles selected for inclusion in the series are highly focused and specific. For example, from the larger category of criminal justice, *Current Controversies* deals with specific topics such as police brutality, gun control, white collar crime, and others. The debates in *Current Controversies* also are presented in a useful, timeless fashion. Articles and book excerpts included in each title are selected if they contribute valuable, long-range ideas to the overall debate. And wherever possible, current information is enhanced with historical documents and other relevant materials. Thus, while individual titles are current in focus, every effort is made to ensure that they will not become quickly outdated. Books in the *Current Controversies* series will remain important resources for librarians, teachers, and students for many years.

In addition to keeping the titles focused and specific, great care is taken in the editorial format of each book in the series. Book introductions and chapter prefaces are offered to provide background material for readers. Chapters are organized around several key questions that are answered with diverse opinions representing all points on the political spectrum. Materials in each chapter include opinions in which authors clearly disagree as well as alternative opinions in which authors may agree on a broader issue but disagree on the possible solutions. In this way, the content of each volume in *Current Controversies* mirrors the mosaic of opinions encountered in society. Readers will quickly realize that there are many viable answers to these complex issues. By questioning each author's conclusions, students and casual readers can begin to develop the critical thinking skills so important to evaluating opinionated material.

Current Controversies is also ideal for controlled research. Each anthology in the series is composed of primary sources taken from a wide gamut of informational categories including periodicals, newspapers, books, U.S. and foreign government documents, and the publications of private and public organizations. Readers will find factual support for reports, debates, and research papers covering all areas of important issues. In addition, an annotated table of contents, an index, a book and periodical bibliography, and a list of organizations to contact are included in each book to expedite further research.

Perhaps more than ever before in history, people are confronted with diverse and contradictory information. During the Persian Gulf War, for example, the public was not only treated to minute-to-minute coverage of the war, it was also inundated with critiques of the coverage and countless analyses of the factors motivating U.S. involvement. Being able to sort through the plethora of opinions accompanying today's major issues, and to draw one's own conclusions, can be a complicated and frustrating struggle. It is the editors' hope that *Current Controversies* will help readers with this struggle.

Introduction

"The fair trade market essentially depends on finding consumers who are willing to pay extra to purchase products that are produced in sustainable ways under fair working conditions."

"Fair trade" (or "fairtrade") is a term that usually refers to an alternate system of trading that exists alongside the conventional, mainstream global trading system of "free trade"—the set of rules and agreements used by most countries to trade with one another. Unlike free trade, which encourages price competition that often lowers the price of goods, fair trade is a system that guarantees a minimum, above-market price to farmers and producers of goods. The purpose of the fair trade movement is to alleviate poverty, provide support to poor people in the developing world, and encourage social and environmental sustainability. As a U.S. fair trade organization explains, "Fair Trade Certification empowers farmers and farm workers to lift themselves out of poverty by investing in their farms and communities, protecting the environment, and developing the business skills necessary to compete in the global marketplace."[1] These ethical standards make products with a fair trade label more costly than similar non-fair-trade products, so the fair trade market essentially depends on finding consumers who are willing to pay extra to purchase products that are produced in sustainable ways under fair working conditions.

The fair trade movement began several decades ago in Europe, when church-related and other relief groups sought to

[1]TransFair USA, "Fair Trade Overview," April 2, 2008. www.transfairusa.org/content/about/overview.php.

help poor communities in developing countries sell their handicrafts to the larger world market. Over time, a variety of alternative trade organizations (ATOs) sprung up not only in Europe but also in the United States and other countries. The first fair trade label was created in 1988 by a Dutch ATO, Solidaridad, to guarantee that its goods met certain labor and environmental standards. The label was called Max Havelaar—named after a character in a nineteenth-century book who opposed the exploitation of coffee workers by Dutch colonial merchants. Other ATOs soon followed suit, each creating their own labels and certification programs. Finally, in 1997, a number of prominent ATOs came together to create the Fairtrade Labelling Organizations International (FLO), an umbrella organization that now has twenty member labeling organizations located in Europe, Canada, the United States, Japan, Australia, and New Zealand. FLO sets uniform fair trade standards, certifies fair trade farmers and producers, and monitors compliance with fair trade standards. The U.S. member of FLO is an organization called TransFair USA. TransFair USA audits fair-trade-certified goods imported by U.S. companies to ensure that farmers and producers are paid fairly and that other fair trade standards are met.

Fair trade standards apply to both producers of goods and to the companies that trade in fair-trade-labeled products. Trader standards require companies wishing to carry fair trade products to pay a fair trade minimum price that covers the costs of sustainable production, as well as an additional premium aimed at helping producers to invest in further development. Traders must also sign contracts that support long-term planning and sustainable production practices and make a partial advance payment, if asked, in order to help small producers get access to capital and to encourage entrepreneurship and development.

Producers, whether small coffee farmers or workers employed by large estates or plantations, must meet certain minimum requirements to become certified, but they also must show progress toward sustainable social, economic, and environmental development. The economic standards require that producers or workers be paid a minimum price for their goods or labor. Environmental standards do not require organic certification, but they do encourage sound agricultural practices like the safe use of chemicals, proper waste management, conservation of soil and water resources, and no use of genetically modified organisms. The social aspect of fair trade standards requires small farmers to create a co-op or similar organization that allows for democratic decision making, operates transparently, and does not discriminate against any particular member or social group. FLO also prohibits child labor, forced labor, and discriminatory labor practices, and it requires minimum occupational safety and health conditions, freedom of association, and access to collective bargaining in the workplace.

Because the underlying goal of fair trade is to benefit disadvantaged farmers and producers in poor nations, most fair trade products are agricultural products that constitute the mainstay export for many developing countries. Early fair trade products tended to be limited to items such as coffee and tea, but today FLO certifies an ever-widening array of products, ranging from rice, sugar, spices, honey, and bananas to flowers, nuts, chocolates, and wine. Recently, manufactured products have also been added to the list of fair-trade-certified products. For example, in 2002, FLO created fair trade standards for sport balls—specifically, soccer balls—as part of an effort to eradicate child labor in the soccer ball industry in Pakistan.

The fair trade market, once considered a tiny niche market, has been growing at a rapid rate in recent years. According to FLO, worldwide consumers spent approximately $2.3 billion on certified products in 2007, a 47 percent increase over the previous year. FLO calculates that the fair trade movement now benefits approximately 1.5 million producers and workers in a total of fifty-eight developing countries in Africa, Asia, and Latin America. The largest growth is occurring in the United Kingdom, where fair trade sales grew a surprising 70 percent in 2007. In addition, fair trade products are increasingly being sold by major retailers such as Starbucks, McDonald's, and Wal-Mart—a trend that some supporters consider a threat to basic fair trade values. Other fair trade advocates want to see fair trade products enter the mainstream and hope to see such products as fair trade coffee, tea, and bananas one day carried by major supermarkets around the world. Supporters compare the fair trade movement to the organic food movement, which eventually grew large enough that governments such as the United States were persuaded to create official government standards.

The fair trade market, however, is still quite small compared to the entire global trading market, and few commentators expect it to replace the current system of global trade. In 2006, for example, only 3.3 percent of coffee sold in the United States was certified fair trade. Yet the ideas embodied in fair trade—such as a fair and living wage for workers, labor standards, and environmental sustainability—are beginning to be demanded by critics of the free trade global trading system, who charge that current global trading rules benefit only the rich, developed countries and their large corporations. Developing countries, in fact, have long complained that the free trade system is not really free, because many industrialized countries have refused to remove agricultural trade barriers and subsidies, thus preventing developing nations from selling their agricultural products fairly on the world market. And in the United States, labor unions and worker advocates often blame free trade for the loss of well-paying jobs, and some are now urging that labor and environmental standards be negotiated as part of existing and future binational or regional trade agreements.

Whether fair trade will continue to grow and ultimately help to change some of the existing injustices in global trade will depend, to a large extent, on the buying trends of millions of consumers as well as the decisions of policy-makers. The authors of viewpoints included in *Current Controversies: Fair Trade* discuss the benefits and the growth patterns of the fair trade market, debate whether fair trade is compatible with free trade, and offer suggestions for how the fair trade system might be improved or how fair trade concepts might be incorporated into the larger global trading system.

CHAPTER 1

Is Fair Trade a Beneficial Policy?

Chapter Preface

In April 2008, Wal-Mart's warehouse-club division, Sam's Club, began selling fair trade coffee, tea, flowers, and bananas. In doing so, Wal-Mart, the world's largest retailer, joined many other large corporations—including Starbucks, McDonald's, and Proctor & Gamble—that have recently sought to cash in on what is a rapidly growing niche market, particularly in the United States and Europe. TransFair USA, the fair trade labeling organization for the United States, has been at the center of this trend toward expanding the fair trade market. Many fair trade advocates support allowing large corporate interests to enter the fair trade market, but the issue has raised concerns among others who think it may dilute the main purposes of fair trade—which are to benefit small, disadvantaged farmers in developing countries; help them to escape poverty; and fund environmentally sustainable development.

Supporters of fair trade expansion to retailers like Wal-Mart see it as a sign of success for the fair trade movement—a step forward from a small, niche market to the larger mass market. If more fair trade goods are sold at the above-market fair trade prices, they reason, more money will be channeled to pay more small farmers, producers, and workers a living wage, and more goods will be produced using sustainable environmental practices. And even if the fair trade benefits go to employees of larger farms rather than to small farmers who band together in co-ops, these fair trade advocates argue, the overall goal of fair trade is achieved because either way, Third World poverty is alleviated and life in developing nations is improved. Advocates of mainstreaming fair trade also note that when fair trade products line the shelves of mass retailers, more consumers will be educated about the fair trade label—possibly creating pressure for more ethical trading practices worldwide. Otherwise, if the fair trade does not expand, it will be forever limited to helping a relative few people in the developing world.

Critics, on the other hand, fear that allowing large corporations into the fair trade market may change the market in undesirable ways, and possibly even undermine its central aim of helping small farmers and producers. The biggest criticism is that the main beneficiaries of the corporate trend are not small farmers but instead large plantations and estates—many of them in Latin America—that have been producing bananas, coffee, and other goods since colonial times. Large plantations have an advantage because large corporations like Wal-Mart prefer to work with mass producers that can supply large amounts of products rather than contracting with dozens of small farmers or co-ops, which would be much less efficient and more difficult. In fact, TransFair USA has attracted vocal criticism for certifying several large plantations as fair trade producers. Commentators say that these fair trade plantations may treat their workers better than other plantations, but the plantation system—run by wealthy owners or large corporations that hire local people simply as employees—is not the type of small-scale development sought by the fair trade movement. Also, there is the issue of whether corporations such as Wal-Mart, which has itself come under widespread criticism for its labor and trading practices, should really become the public face of fair trade.

In addition, many critics question whether it is possible for TransFair USA or other fair trade organizations to effectively monitor wages and labor standards on large estates and plantations situated in foreign countries that have no tradition of labor unions, workers' rights, or environmental protections. Such an effort, they say, would likely require significant resources well beyond the ability of existing fair trade monitoring groups. Absent such effective oversight, critics worry that fair trade plantations will likely return to traditional practices, which kept workers low paid, non-union, and afraid to make demands. Already, some news reports have surfaced claiming that workers in some large fair-trade-certified estates and plantations are not receiving the benefits promised by the fair trade label.

The issue of moving fair trade products into the mainstream lies at the root of many of the controversies surrounding the fair trade market. If the fair trade market stays small, critics complain that it benefits only a relative few people, but the risk is that as the market grows, its standards and benefits may be diluted or co-opted by larger market forces. The viewpoints in this chapter explore this issue as well as others related to the basic question of whether fair trade is a beneficial policy.

Fair Trade Helps to Transform the Lives of Poor Farmers

Rachel Dixon

Rachel Dixon is a correspondent for The Guardian, *a British newspaper.*

Does buying Fairtrade products really make a difference to people's lives? Rachel Dixon talks to three producers and finds out how their communities have been transformed.

Gerardo Arias Camacho, Coffee Producer, Costa Rica

Gerardo is a coffee farmer in Llano Bonito, San José, Costa Rica. He is a board member on his village cooperative, which is a member of the Fairtrade consortium COOCAFE. He is married with three children.

In the 1980s, the price of coffee fell so low that it didn't cover the cost of production. Many farmers abandoned their land and went to the cities to find work. Some even left the country. In the mid-90s, I decided to go to America to make money and support my family. After eight years, I had earned enough to buy the family farm so that my parents could retire. But coffee prices were still so low that I was forced to go back to the States for another two years.

The coffee market was so unstable. We did not have a local school, good roads or bridges. Now that our consortium is Fairtrade certified, prices are stable and we receive a guaranteed premium. We spend the money on education, environmental protection, roads and bridges, and improving the old processing plant. We have sponsored a scholarship programme so that our kids can stay in school.

I believe that my cooperative would be out of business if it wasn't for Fairtrade. Free trade is not responsible trade. When prices go down, farmers produce more and prices drop further. Fairtrade is the way trade should be: fair, responsible and sustainable.

Since Fairtrade, our farms have become more environmentally friendly.

My oldest son is in college, my ten-year-old has already had as much education as me, and my little princess is in her second year at school. With the help of Fairtrade, they might all be able to go to university and get a degree. They won't have to jump the border from Mexico to America, leaving the country for ten years, like me. They can decide what they want in life. I tell them: 'You have two choices. You can be a coffee grower or you can be something else. But learn how to be a coffee grower first, like your father and your grandfather.'

Since Fairtrade, our farms have become more environmentally friendly. Our coffee is now produced in a sustainable way. We have planted trees and reduced the use of pesticides by 80% in 10 years. We used to cut 20 hectares (50 acres) of forest down every year to fuel the ovens at our processing plant. Now we have a new oven which is fuelled by waste products, including coffee skins and the skins of macadamia nuts that we buy from farmers on the other side of Costa Rica. It is a win-win business.

Fairtrade is not a closed system, it is open to everyone. But we need more and more people to buy Fairtrade so that the market grows and other farmers can become certified. Fairtrade can be a tool to help farmers who are not certified. We educate the producers around us about market prices so that buyers have to offer them a competitive rate. It also benefits the wider community. When there was a hurricane, the new road became blocked and the bridge came down. We could afford to open the road and fix the bridge.

When you are shopping, look for the Fairtrade label—you can be sure that the money is going straight to the producers. It will help us, but it will also help people around the world, because the benefits of protecting the environment are for everyone. It is a matter of helping each other.

As a Fairtrade farmer, I finally feel competitive—I feel that I have a tool in my hand. It has given me knowledge, so that I am more able to defend myself and my people. I feel there is a future in front of us, because we can stay in our own country and make a living growing coffee.

Fairtrade is not charity. Just by going shopping, you can make a difference.

Julius Ethang'atha, Tea Producer, Kenya

Julius is a retired tea producer from Michimikuru, Kenya. He helped to introduce Fairtrade tea production to Kenya five years ago, while working for the Kenya Tea Development Agency (KTDA).

Africa does not need aid; we need to participate in a fairer trading system. Teach us how to fish—do not just give us the fish.

You can't keep all your eggs in the same basket, so we try many things in Kenya. I tried tea. When I was working for the KTDA, buyers asked for Fairtrade. It wasn't easy to become certified, but I saw it was the best way out for our people.

There was a huge impact on the first communities to work with Fairtrade. They were poor communities; they did not have water, dispensaries or schools close to them. The money they got from tea was used for food and clothes, but now they also get a premium that they can use to improve their social living. So far they have set up impressive schools and daycare centres, dispensaries, maternity units, water systems, bridges and roads.

I think criticism of Fairtrade is ridiculous. Yes, Fairtrade only accounts for a small share of the cake, but it is growing. Saying 'Do not buy Fairtrade, because it doesn't help non-Fairtrade producers' is like saying 'Do not eat, because others are hungry'.

Africa does not need aid; we need to participate in a fairer trading system. Teach us how to fish—do not just give us the fish. You see, the farmer receives just 5% of the wealth in tea. When the consumer pays more for Fairtrade tea, this extra money goes to the farmer and improves lives. But if the whole value chain was made fairer, Africa would be lifted out of poverty.

Fairtrade is the right way to shop. It puts a smile on the faces of children in Africa, and it makes their lives bearable.

Makandianfing Keita, Cotton Farmer, Mali

Makandianfing is a cotton farmer in Dougourakoroni village, Mali, west Africa. The village cotton farmers are members of the UC-CPC de Djidian cooperative, which has been Fairtrade-certified since 2005. Makandianfing married last year.

Cotton prices were going down and down until they were below the cost of production. People were demotivated and it was very depressing. But now, we can make a sustainable living. My family can eat and we have better health.

In the past, children had to walk 10km to go to school, so really it was impossible. We have now been able to build a school. At first it had two classrooms. When we had more money and wanted to expand, we challenged the government to match our investment. Now there are five classrooms in total, and every child in the village can go to school.

Pregnant women had no access to healthcare. Many died in childbirth and there were high rates of infant mortality.

Now we have built a maternity centre. We have also built a food storage facility so that we can have a year-round food supply, and we have installed a pump for drinking water. We have built a new road, enabling us to travel further than 5km outside of the village without difficulty.

Fairtrade standards called for better agricultural practices. Before, empty pesticide containers would be used as water carriers. In some cases this led to death. Now, we dispose of waste properly. We don't burn bushes any more, we prevent soil erosion and we have effective irrigation.

Fairtrade has really changed the life of my community. I feel as though I have a future, which I didn't before. My wife is pregnant with our first child—this is how optimistic we are!

I encourage everyone to buy more Fairtrade products if they want to make an impact on millions of lives.

Fair Trade Is Effective and Rewarding

Anne O'Loughlin

Anne O'Loughlin is the president and founder of Autonomie Project, a new fair trade fashion and footwear company in Boston, Massachusetts.

With the beginning of October [2008] comes the official kick off to Fair Trade Month, a month-long celebration and promotion of Fair Trade-certified products. Indeed, the Fair Trade movement has a lot to celebrate this year. According to the Fair Trade Labelling Organization International (FLO), consumers around the world spent more than $3 billion on Fair Trade-certified items in 2007, a whopping increase of 47% from the previous year! An increasing amount of diverse products [is] also entering the Fair Trade market, thus expanding consumers' options from the traditionally known Fair Trade items such as crafts, coffee, and chocolate to include fruits, wine, flowers and even soccer balls and shoes. This means that now over 1.5 million producers and workers in approximately 58 developing countries can benefit from increased business due to Fair Trade sales.

Criticisms of Fair Trade

It's been commonly understood that Fair Trade is a preferable, more moral way of conducting business than the conventional 'top down' approach of major, multi-national corporations in which sweatshops tend to thrive and the workers on the lowest levels are squeezed. The underlying principles of Fair Trade are to deliver more than just a financial package to the workers, in order to not only guarantee that they are paid a fair rate/wage but also to create a system in which a long-term, sustainable relationship is developed between the buyer and third world producers that will ultimately empower these workers and their community to thrive and succeed in the global marketplace

In recent months, however, some organizations have doubted the true benefit of Fair Trade and have started to question the validity and impact of the movement. On February 25[, 2008], Britain's economic think tank The Adam Smith Institute, a self-proclaimed leading innovator of free-market economic and social policies, published a report by Marc Sidwell entitled *Unfair Trade*. Mr. Sidwell argues that Fair Trade is actually anything but fair and while Fair Trade and its supporters may have positive intentions, it actually does more harm than good.

Sidwell writes that Fair Trade distorts local markets by fixing a high price of goods for only a small percentage of producers (thus hurting the majority of the other farmers producing the same goods at lower costs who are allegedly excluded from Fair Trade business practices). He also argues that Fair Trade is "irrelevant" to large scale poverty relief and does not aid economic development properly—rather, it prevents the poor from gaining the proper tools to successfully improve their financial outlook. He goes on to claim that Fair Trade actually prevents farmers from advancing their technologies and efficiencies and the opportunity for diversification, and are thus actually stuck in an *un*sustainable practice.

Sidwell furthermore asserts that Fair Trade is merely a marketing scheme that rewards inefficient farmers who produce poor-quality goods, thus also being unfair to . . . consumer[s] who allegedly [have] a wealth of ethical purchasing options available to them without even knowing it due to the overwhelming monopoly of Fair Trade-certified goods.

The Truth About Fair Trade

As would be expected, the release of this report caused a backlash of responses from the Fair Trade community and ethical bloggers alike, including a lengthy, evidence-driven press release from The Fairtrade Foundation [that attempted] to discredit Sidwell's arguments. They angrily write, "Two billion people work extremely hard to earn a living but still earn less than $2 per day and the FAIRTRADE Mark enables consumers to choose products that help address this injustice. As no-one is forced to join a fair trade producer organisation, or to buy Fairtrade products, you would think that free market economists like the Adam Smith Institute would be pleased at the way the public has taken our voluntary label to its heart . . ."

So how is Fair Trade really affecting the workers of the world and is its global impact truly innovative and revolutionary, or merely smoke and mirrors as Mr. Sidwell points out?

The world needs . . . a harmonious balance between Free and Fair Trade in which poor nations on a macro level and lower class workers on a micro level can all flourish.

After spending 17 solid pages tearing the Fair Trade mission into pieces, Sidwell's only suggestion for a viable alternative is to follow the global path of Free Trade. He uses China and India as two examples of how Free Trade has lifted traditionally poverty-stricken countries into more solid financial positions where they very recently have been successfully lobbying for global economic leadership positions. While Sidwell's examples may offer some element of truth, it certainly does not account for the long list of human rights abuses and exploits both countries have added to their economic repertoires.

With a debate like this, we have to stop and ask ourselves is the explosive growth of China and India truly having a proper "trickle down" effect? That is, are the workers of the world, the people at the lowest level, the people that bear the brunt of globalization on their backs really feeling any kind of financial relief or reward from the macro economic improvements of their nations? And what about the workers living in countries that are not advantageously growing with globalization, such as Peru, Argentina, Ethiopia, Haiti . . . the list goes on? Do they have no opportunity for growth . . . or can the Fair Trade market act as an outlet for these workers to exit the fringes and become active players in the global marketplace? Perhaps what the world needs is a harmonious balance between Free and Fair Trade in which poor nations on a macro level and lower class workers on a micro level can all flourish together. After all, with a happy, healthy workforce comes increased loyalty, ownership and productivity which ultimately trickles *up* to the overall economic growth of the nation as a whole.

Regardless of anyone's argument, I can tell you that after personally experiencing close contact with real people in the developing world, doing business under Fair Trade principles is a rewarding and effective method of trade. It provides wonderful opportunity to meet, get to know, and partner directly with the people that are actually making our products. I see firsthand how our business affects and improves their lives, the lives of their families and their community. And hear the passion, excitement and pride in their voices when they receive a new order. Maybe I missed something . . . but to us, this is what Fair Trade is all about.

Fair Trade Can Help Stop Global Warming

Zarah Patriana

Zarah Patriana is the operations manager for the Global Exchange Fair Trade Online Store, a project of the international human rights organization Global Exchange.

Can Fair Trade stop global warming? One of the main tenets of Fair Trade is environmental sustainability, so while it is not the sole solution to the problem, it is offering one of many solutions to alleviate the problem of climate change. So, how is Fair Trade doing this? Let us count the ways.

Traditional Farming Techniques

In the so-called 'Green' Revolution of the 1970s, the US Agency for International Development and others gave millions of dollars to Central American farmers to replace traditional shade grown farming techniques with 'sun cultivation' to increase coffee yields. This meant an increased use of chemicals and pesticides, cutting down of trees and monocropping, which essentially led to the severe destruction of forests and the biodiversity of over 1.1 million hectares and also the extinction of songbirds.

To counter this destruction, the Fair Trade movement addresses the situation with the farmers' interests and their local ecosystem in mind. Small farmers were seeing the destruction around them and, knowing the value of the land, were determined to see their land survive for future generations.

Over 80% of Fair Trade-Certified coffee is shade grown, preserving crucial habitat for migratory birds, plants, insects and animals. In a study by Mario Bolanos Mendez, he found sixty identifiable plants, more than one hundred bird species, several reptile species and mammals in a few sample shade-grown coffee plots.

Sustainability is the name of the [Fair Trade] game.

Over 60% of Fair Trade Certified coffee is also certified Organic, requiring the farmers to use non-chemical methods of pest management. Fair Trade farmers also implement soil and conservation methods such as reforestation, terracing and composting.

Environmental Sustainability

The work that Fair Trade does with small-scale producers is a step toward reducing our environmental footprint. As Equal Exchange points out:

> [T]he sustainable farming practices of small-scale producers actually help cool the planet, protect the environment, and restore local ecosystems. Organic farming, reforestation, soil and watershed protection, and the use of stoves that convert organic waste into methane gas are just some of the ways in which small-scale farmers are keeping our food, our bodies, and our ecosystems healthy. By supporting small-scale farmers, we can bring justice to the food system and help reduce the effects of our changing climate. It's a win-win solution that benefits us all.

Sustainability is the name of the game. More reasons behind the benefits of Fair Trade on the environment? The Fair Trade Resource Network gives you five along with stories from those in the Fair Trade movement and their work to alleviate the problem of climate change.

The Fair Trade movement explores different solutions to various problems facing us today, such as global warming. While it may not be the sole solution, Fair Trade movement proves that business and trade can put the environment and people before profit. As environmental activist Vandana Shiva once said about Fair Trade: "Fair Trade is . . . the practice of what trade should really look like if it has to serve the earth, protect farmers, protect our biodiversity, and protect our cultural diversity."

The Fair Trade Movement Has Begun to Challenge Injustices in the Global Trading System

Zarrin T. Caldwell

Zarrin T. Caldwell is an editor for OneWorld.net, *an online media gateway for independently produced news on a host of issues that impact people worldwide.*

Approximately half the labor force in 120 developing countries depend on agriculture to earn enough to support their families. Besides the hard physical labor these individuals endure on a daily basis, they face a global system in which producers in wealthy countries are able to sell goods at artificially low prices, thanks to subsidies provided by their governments. Having to deal with these and other barriers to trade, as well as the whims of sometimes unstable world markets, many in the developing world are finding that the labors their families have engaged in for generations simply no longer pay. But, there is an alternative for some.

In an effort to try to account for some of the disadvantages faced by the poor, a global "fair trade" movement has arisen, which . . . has begun to ensure a fair and living wage for producers of certain specialized products in the global South. Incomes from the sale of fair trade products, which are often managed by cooperatives, have also been used to improve educational and health services in many rural communities. The reality remains, however, that while the fair trade movement has made a positive difference in the lives of many, it represents only a minor fraction of a global trading system that many believe is unjust.

Zarrin T. Caldwell, "Global Trade: Free or Fair?" *OneWorld.net*, November 29, 2005. Reproduced by permission. OneWorld.net is an online hub for people who care about the world beyond their own borders.

Defining "Free" Trade

The modern world largely operates under a so-called free trade system. Those advocating for this system note that benefits of trade will accrue to the most people when a government interferes as little as possible with imports and exports and lets the supply and demand of markets work freely to set prices. In theory, if a country or region is using its labor pool and natural resources to specialize in the development of a product or service, such specialization will lead to greater efficiency, higher production, and benefits for everyone. If free trade is operating as it should, then the job creation that results can be an important force in improving the lives of the poor.

Providing government subsidies to the agricultural sector ... is a common practice, particularly in wealthier countries.

But, is free trade really "free"? Free trade is so named because it means that goods and services should be traded without tariffs imposed by governments or the use of other trade barriers like quotas, which limit the volume of imports into a country. It means that there will be a minimum of restraints when foreign companies want to invest directly in domestic plants and equipment. And, it also means that certain industries will not get government financial help, or subsidies, in order to sell their goods at below-market prices. In short, it means that domestic industries get no special favors and, like everyone else, have to compete in an open international marketplace.

In reality though, such an ideal rarely exists. Both developed and developing countries engage in different kinds of trade restrictions like those mentioned above. In efforts to protect favored domestic industries, for example, governments will often place high tariffs or import quotas on the goods produced by similar foreign industries that are trying to access their markets. Wealthier countries are naturally better positioned to protect their industries than poorer countries are.

Subsidies Considered

Providing government subsidies to the agricultural sector—often in the form of cash payments to farmers producing a particular crop or raising certain animals—is a common practice, particularly in wealthier countries. Producers of rice, sugar, milk, wheat, grains, meats, and other agricultural products in OECD (Organization of Economic Cooperation and Development) countries—which include the U.S., EU [European Union], Australia, Japan, and Canada, among others—received $279 billion in total support in 2004, according to a recent report. The developing world has consistently criticized such countries—with the European Union [members] taking particular heat—for the generous financial support they provide to their farmers. Such subsidies give farmers in the developed world a definite advantage, but result in driving down prices on world markets. In a practice known as "dumping," products are exported to other countries at an unfairly low price, which makes the fruits of poor country farmers' labor much less profitable. Many advocating for fair trade have called for the abolition of such agricultural subsidies. Other fair trade groups point to historical trade inequalities, noting that if any farmers should be subsidized it should be those in poor countries.

Some of this pressure may be working, as producer support in most of these countries has gradually declined over the past 20 years. As the above-noted report indicates, however, levels of support remain high, and large differences exist across countries. Despite the media focus on agricultural subsidies in the U.S., support to U.S. producers in 2002–2004 was 20 percent of farm receipts, whereas this figure was 60 percent in Japan and 70 percent in countries like Switzerland and

Norway. Smaller countries do not have as much impact on global prices as does the U.S. Still, if the U.S. is being pressured to make large cuts in trade-distorting support for agriculture, it wants to see other countries do the same. Although many fair trade advocates remain skeptical that market access will improve for heavily protected industries like sugar and dairy, the U.S. and the EU have recently voiced commitments to begin phasing in substantial reductions to support measures and tariffs over several years. At the same time, they want developing countries to open their doors to more trade in industrial goods and services. Of course, developing countries do not provide anything like the levels of subsidies that developed countries do and, hence, their impact on global prices is much less than that of the U.S. and EU.

> *From the point of view of many developing countries . . . current trade rules serve the interests of wealthier nations and the big corporations based within them.*

Poor Countries Weigh in

Finding strength in numbers, a group of developing countries formed a coalition called the G20 to negotiate trade concessions at the last Ministerial Conference of the World Trade Organization (WTO)—the primary decision-making forum for the global trading system—held in Cancun, Mexico, in September 2003. Led by India, China, Brazil, South Africa, and Argentina, the G20 called for the U.S., the EU, and Japan to reduce import tariffs and domestic subsidies—especially in agriculture—so that developing nations would have more market access. For many years, groups of developing countries have also lobbied for trade preferences that take account of their disadvantaged position in the global marketplace. Although such preferences can often give these countries space to compete internationally, critics cite their complexity, politicization, and trade-distorting effects and, thus, they remain very controversial.

In the meantime, industrialized countries have wanted developing countries to further open their markets to foreign companies. They also remain concerned about the impacts that low-cost goods from overseas might have on domestic jobs. Disagreements over all of these points led to a breakdown of global trade talks at Cancun. While promises have since been made by wealthier governments that farm subsidies would be reduced, the outcome of the next important Ministerial Conference—taking place December 13–18 [2005] in Hong Kong—remains to be determined [in November 2005]. Developing countries have, nonetheless, made it clear that they want and expect a meaningful role in the discussions.

The Views of Developing Countries

From the point of view of many developing countries—and most civil society organizations—current trade rules serve the interests of wealthier nations and the big corporations based within them. And, not only in agriculture. Intellectual property rights, for example, tend to favor large software and pharmaceutical companies in the North, they argue.

The fair trade movement has sought to challenge inequalities in the international marketplace by linking ethical consumers . . . with organized groups of producers.

As the most influential world forum on trade policy, the WTO is the central target of some non-governmental organizations (NGOs), which see the organization as catering to rich country interests at the expense of the poor. Organizations such as Focus on the Global South, the "Our World Is Not for Sale" Network, and Global Exchange are among NGOs that claim the WTO increases poverty, is a tool of powerful lobbies, and does not have democratic decision-making processes. The WTO refutes such accusations, adding that decisions are made by consensus, that the WTO is only a forum for member states, and that over three-quarters of WTO members are developing or least developed countries. Although organizations like Oxfam try to influence the direction of WTO negotiations, other civil society groups have called for scrapping the WTO altogether and lobby for working through an institution like the U.N. Conference on Trade and Development, which is seen to be more sensitive to developing country concerns.

Whatever position they may take on the WTO, civil society groups are consistent in their message that, with a fairer trading system, significant numbers of people could escape poverty. In its "Make Trade Fair" campaign, for example, Oxfam notes that "if Africa, East Asia, South Asia, and Latin America were each to increase their share of world exports by one percent, the resulting gains in income could lift 128 million people out of poverty." Anti-poverty campaigners such as Oxfam further assert that trade barriers cost poor countries twice as much as they receive in foreign aid.

For all of these reasons, many fair trade campaigners have made "trade not aid" their central theme. Above all, the fair trade movement has sought to challenge inequalities in the international marketplace by linking ethical consumers in the North more directly with organized groups of producers in the South. This movement may not be an answer to all of the perceived injustices in the global trading system, but many see it as an important start.

Fair Trade Is Unfair to Most Poor Farmers

Marc Sidwell

Marc Sidwell is a writer and a research fellow for the New Culture Forum, a Web site of conservative views.

Fairtrade promotes itself in Britain as the only ethical labelling system worth considering. That attitude is plain in [Fairtrade Foundation] director's [Harriet Lamb] new book, . . . published in 2008, but it seems to be a longstanding position.

The Fairtrade insistence that it does not oversee a system of charitable transfer helps to maintain the moral pressure on consumers (fair-dealing is compulsory for honourable people; charity is only voluntary) but it is hard to identify the difference between a direct charitable payment to a coffee community and the extra income provided by Fairtrade. Given the relative inefficiencies of obtaining money by maintaining an international certification scheme, the main difference would seem to be that direct charitable transfers would be far larger. In any case, the essential concern is that the Fairtrade Foundation discourages individuals from even exploring other options, which may well be more effective. . . .

Where Is the Evidence?

The Fairtrade Foundation website reveals that little original research has been produced on the merits and effectiveness of the Fairtrade approach to fighting poverty. Indeed. What research there is appears to be somewhat out-of-date. Given the ever-changing nature of global markets, this may create a misleading impression.

Marc Sidwell, "Unfair Trade," London: *Adam Smith Institute*, 2008. © Adam Smith Research Trust 2007. Reproduced by permission.

As Philip Booth and Linda Whetstone point out in "Half a Cheer for Fair Trade," the 1997/2002 coffee report, "Spilling the Beans" particularly guilty of this:

> [M]any of the arguments within the paper have been completely undermined by developments within the market since that time.

Even where Fairtrade can improve conditions locally for some farmers, it will impose a high cost on others who may be even more deserving.

Instead of hard evidence, Fairtrade advocates usually rely on anecdotes of farmers happy to be part of Fairtrade—perhaps a tacit admission that statistics would be too revealing. These stories may be persuasive and emotionally appealing to the unguarded public, but they do not answer the very real questions about the effectiveness of the Fairtrade model.

A Question of Trust

The continuing expansion of the Fairtrade Mark in the UK [United Kingdom] rests on public trust in the Fairtrade idea. Yet on closer examination, the concept's positive image appears to rely more on public relations than research.

There are a number of awkward facts about Fairtrade that the public will not easily discover from Fairtrade publicity.

Fairtrade makes some farmers worse off.

As the Mexican example shows, even where Fairtrade can improve conditions locally for some farmers, it will impose a high cost on others who may be even more deserving. Fairtrade must pick among farmers on the basis of whether they are able to bring a buyer to the table and whether they meet Fairtrade standards, not on the basis of need. They must exclude some equally deserving cases. And those who fall outside the Fairtrade regime may then find themselves worse off thanks to Fairtrade, either through international competition, or because Fairtrade segments the market, creating a parallel "exploitation coffee" sector, as the economist Tyler Cowen has suggested, or because protection of one area of the market weakens the position of the rest, as Philip Booth has argued:

> What happens if there is adjustment to world supply or demand and prices in one part of the market are fixed? Prices in other parts of the market must fall by more—others suffer. What happens to employees of large producers when fair trade consumption shifts away from them towards small producers? They may have no alternative employment.

According to some estimates, Mexico produces 25% of Fairtrade coffee. Mexico has the largest number of Fairtrade certified producer organisations in the world: fifty-one. The whole of India has just forty-nine; South Africa has thirty-eight; Colombia has thirty-four. Most of the subsistence economies that people think of as central to Fairtrade have far, far fewer. Burundi has no Fairtrade certified producers; Ethiopia has four; Rwanda has ten. In Ethiopia, 80% of the population work in agriculture, with an average income of $700 a year. In Mexico, 18% work in the fields, and the average salary is $9000. In practice, then, Fairtrade pays to support relatively wealthy Mexican coffee farmers at the expense of the poorer nations.

Fairtrade is an inefficient way to transfer money, with 90% of the premium going to retailers.

Most Fairtrade-certified crops are not in Fairtrade products.

For a producer, Fairtrade certification guarantees a fixed Fairtrade price, but not the proportion of any crop that will be bought at Fairtrade prices. It is hard to know exactly how little Fairtrade-certified produce is sold for Fairtrade prices, but FLO International estimates just 20%. Harriet Lamb [director of the Fairtrade Foundation] refers to a producer who is glad to see it reach 15%, having at one time only sold 5% of his crop at Fairtrade prices.

Since most Fairtrade crops are not sold at Fairtrade prices, the price-fixing regime is far less generous than it sounds, especially as farms must make expensive adjustments to all their working practices and pay certification fees just to qualify. Fairtrade also becomes a worse deal for the consumer, as farmers can sell their best beans on the free market and collect the fixed Fairtrade rate for their worst produce.

Just 10% of the premium paid for Fairtrade coffee reaches the producer.

While it may still be true that the money reaching a farming cooperative via Fairtrade will be significant to them, Fairtrade is an inefficient way to transfer money, with 90% of the premium paid going to retailers. Given that the consumer very likely pays the large Fairtrade premium on the understanding that it is a direct charitable contribution, they would be willing to send far more to poor farmers than farmers receive through the Fairtrade certification process. The Fairtrade tendency to discourage individuals from donating directly to charities arguably draws them away from the most efficient way to give, in favour of Fairtrade, losing the producers money.

It is hard to conclude that Fairtrade does much good and, indeed, it may even do some harm.

Fairtrade is irrelevant.

Sales of Fair Trade coffee do not make up more than 5% of the coffee market in any consuming country.

In the Fairtrade literature, the emphasis is on their extraordinary rate of growth, with sales growing 40% year on year. Yet these increases are taking place from such a low base that the market share continues to remain irrelevant to large-scale poverty relief. We can see this in another way by observing how Fairtrade is rapidly diversifying into new product lines. This is because it is much easier to take a small proportion of sales in many different kinds of produce than to seriously increase market share in one. Fairtrade bananas, one of Fairtrade's greatest success stories, account for just one in every five bananas sold in the UK. However, in the process of diversifying, any negative consequences of Fairtrade will be multiplied across many different kinds of producer, without resolving the problem that Fairtrade cannot be a large-scale answer to producer poverty. In fact, the alternative labelling schemes such as the Rainforest Alliance may well do more good simply because they are adopted by large corporations and are put into effect on a much wider basis.

The Fair Trade movement has a political agenda.

At times, the wider Fair Trade movement admit that retail Fairtrade is not intended to be the answer to poverty it is commonly understood as, but the softening-up exercise to a sweeping alteration in the rules of global commerce and the attempted control and management of production and trade. [According to Lamb:]

> Fairtrade turns the tact that we all go shopping into a new tactic for us to act together to tell those who run trade, that we not only don't like the way they do it at the moment, but we want them to back a fairer alternative.

> Fairtrade also plays a more practical role in building a broad-based movement for change . . . Fairtrade is an easy way in . . . It helps give our governments a mandate to take the big, bold steps needed to change world trade rules.

Do most consumers realize that the real value of their Fairtrade purchase is considered to lie in the weight it adds to a campaign to radically remake the international economic order? Surely not. In fact, even economists sometimes point to

Fairtrade as an example of voluntary market exchange that should not be gainsaid by free trade enthusiasts. Like most consumers, they do not recognise the antipathy to free market principles that lies beneath the consumer friendly packaging.

The Fair Trade movement undoubtedly means well, and its supporters truly believe that buying Fairtrade products helps to reduce developing world poverty. Unfortunately, closer investigation reveals, that this is not the case. On a dispassionate analysis, it is hard to conclude that Fairtrade does much good and, indeed, it may even do some harm. Certainly, were the Fair Trade movement to realize its broader political objectives, the cause of international development would be severely compromised. . . . Consumers surely deserve to know these awkward truths, so that that they can make genuinely informed decisions in the goods they buy and the charities they support.

Many Workers at Fair-Trade-Certified Tea Estates Do Not Receive Fair Trade Benefits

Parminder Bahra

Parminder Bahra is poverty and development correspondent for The Times, *a newspaper in the United Kingdom.*

Supermarkets seeking to promote their ethical buying policies proclaim that their produce is Fairtrade, and customers buy such goods in the belief that they are doing their bit for workers in the developing world.

However, an investigation by *The Times* suggests that workers on plantations that supply Fairtrade tea are not seeing their lives improve as they should.

Some workers suspect that the scheme is being used to make estates appear socially responsible as demand increases in the West for Fairtrade-labelled goods.

Sales of Fairtrade produce command a premium that is supposed to be used for the benefit of estate workers. It should be passed to them through a committee of managers and workers who decide where and how it is spent.

Managers at one tea estate in Kenya said that Fairtrade regulations were too expensive or difficult to implement and that some of their workers found them too restrictive. At an estate in India, Fairtade inspectors found problems with the way that the premium was managed and many workers complained that they had seen no benefit.

Some workers suspect that the scheme is being used to make estates appear socially responsible as demand increases in the West for Fairtrade-labelled goods.

Fairtrade has grown from a small nongovernmental organisation to a global enterprise, with 21 international bodies—including the Fairtrade Foundation in Britain—under the umbrella of the Fairtrade Labelling Organisation (FLO), which sets the standards for certification. Estates are checked and certificates awarded by FLO-CERT, which FLO says is independent but wholly owned by FLO.

Certification allows an estate to sell tea labelled as Fairtrade, but it is up to wholesalers to decide whether to buy the tea as Fairtrade—or more cheaply as standard tea without the label. Fairtrade estates can also supplement their output by buying from noncertified plantations, although they cannot then sell such produce as Fairtrade. For example, Eastern Produce Kenya, a Fairtrade-certified trader, regularly buys noncertified tea from the Kaprachoge estate, where conditions are far from those stipulated for certification.

Problems with the Fairtrade Certification System

Tom Heinemann, a Danish film-maker, visited more than 20 estates in India, Sri Lanka, Bangladesh and Kenya for his documentary *The Bitter Taste of Tea*. He found few workers who had benefited from the premium. "Workers get things like a gas cylinder, a Thermos flask or a laundry basket. But these would come after years of not getting anything," he said.

Mr Heinemann also said that the Fairtrade inspections are announced in advance. "The estate owners can tell the workers not to be critical. It is a harsh system—[the workers] are deeply afraid of the owners because they can lose their job[s]."

In Kenya, Mr Heinemann says that it is common to find workers hired for three months, fired and later rehired to avoid laws that would oblige owners to hire workers full-time.

Paola Ghillani, the former chief executive of the Max Havelaar Foundation in Switzerland, the Swiss version of Fairtrade, and a former board member of FLO, says: "The Fairtrade label has grown so fast, but has forgotten to invest enough in growth management like normal companies."

While at FLO, she found herself at odds with the Fairtrade Foundation in Britain. The foundation was unhappy with inspections being conducted by independent organisations and it tried to influence the outcomes of these inspections, she said.

"The Fairtrade Foundation at that time, and maybe now, has got too much at stake. They were living from funding, but also from licence fees [they received] each time they gave the label to a licensee. The inspection and certification system is not independent enough."

Despite reservations, Ms Ghillani is still supportive. "Fairtrade labelling is an inspiring instrument," she said.

Denials from FLO

The Fairtrade Foundation denies that inspections are not professional. It claims that FLO-CERT is independent and meets the requirements of ISO 65 [an International Standards Organization guideline], the international quality standard for certification bodies.

It also rejects the claim that workers do not benefit. A spokeswoman said: "Before becoming Fairtrade-certified, estates need to demonstrate that they meet Fairtrade standards to pay decent wages, guarantee the right to join a trade union, ensure health and safety standards, and provide adequate housing and other social provision where relevant.

"Educating workers about Fairtrade and the premium is an ongoing process. It is incumbent on management to make sure staff are aware of Fairtrade. However, where Fairtrade sales are low, management and the joint body can feel it is not fair to raise too much expectation of the Fairtrade premium."

Retailers May Benefit the Most from Fair Trade

Frances Stead Sellers

Frances Stead Sellers is an assistant editor of Outlook, *a Sunday publication of* The Washington Post.

Earlier this month, there was a three-day sale of imported Oriental rugs at the Mennonite church near my house in Baltimore. "They *are* a little pricey," one of my neighbors warned me wryly, "because the workers are paid a living wage." What a concept! The last time I bought an Oriental rug—years ago in Kashmir—I haggled over the price with little thought for the well-being of the rugmakers. I was pretty sure most of the profit would go to the store owner, anyway. But now my already stressful shopping season—garlanded with aspirations to find creative presents—had been complicated by the intrusion of altruism: I was meant to worry about the workers.

So it was that I found myself watching another neighbor sort through piles of richly patterned, hand-knotted rugs, looking for just the right ruby tone to replace the threadbare floor covering in her dining room. She knew she probably wouldn't get a bargain that day, but she had been persuaded by the saleswoman's spiel that there was added ethical value to her purchase: Her investment would support Pakistani craftsmen and women (but no children, of course) who use looms donated by a charity, Jakciss, that is committed to building schools and promoting harmony between the country's Christian and Muslim populations.

I left the church with a warm feeling about an organization that was helping to maintain village life half a world away. But without a rug.

Buying a pricey Oriental would have been beyond my budget, I told myself, and was not, therefore, the right thing for me to do. I'd check out some cheaper handcrafts instead, and other goods sold to support traditional artisans and farmers in the developing world. That decision pitched me, wallet-first, into the moral minefield of the movement known as "ethical shopping."

Using buying power to improve the world is a growing commitment among consumers in this country, according to the rug sellers at the Mennonite church, who told me that increasing numbers of customers ask well-informed questions about the conditions under which their purchases had been made. And it has become big business in Europe, where a fair trade consumer guarantee was launched almost 20 years ago under the Dutch label Max Havelaar. The aim back then was to replicate the moral mindset that charities like Jakciss had fostered around niche handcraft markets and take it mainstream. According to the umbrella group Fairtrade Labelling Organizations International (FLO), there are now fair trade initiatives in 20 countries, including the United States, for such staples as cocoa, chocolate bars, orange juice, tea, honey, sugar and bananas as well as the ur-currency of the fair trade world—coffee. Between 2002 and 2003, sales of these goods grew by 42.3 percent worldwide. But there is also controversy brewing about just who's profiting from the guilt-charged spending habits of the Western world's consumers.

Conservative commentator Philip Oppenheim . . . argued recently that in Britain, it's supermarkets that profit most from fair trade sales.

The pervasiveness of those habits came home to me a couple of months ago when I was in Britain (the world's largest fair trade market). My usually frugal brother sought out ground decaf coffee with the distinctive green and blue Fairtrade logo—and a higher price tag—for me at the Sainsbury's supermarket. Matthew told me he's prepared to pay more for fair trade "if a couple of pennies go to the poor grower," and he also tries to support people who grow produce locally in Cornwall, where he lives. But, he says, he's not holier-than-thou about his shopping, and he sometimes finds that his two goals conflict. He'll cast an eye over the ethical shopping reports that appear in London's newspapers now that the movement has picked up enough steam to cater regularly to people like him. The liberal *Guardian* reviews the Ethical Consumer Research Association's "best buys," which allocates each purer-than-the-driven-snow product a numerical "ethiscore."

The knowledge that people like my brother will pick fair trade products first off the supermarket shelves has prompted many stores to advertise the fact that they stock fair trade foods. And that has led, others suggest, to an indigestible melange of entrepreneurship and ethics.

That, at least, is the contention of conservative commentator Philip Oppenheim, who argued recently that in Britain, it's supermarkets that profit most from fair trade sales. They charge a premium for fair trade bananas, for example, while a "minuscule sliver ends up with the people the movement is designed to help," he writes. I'm not sure whether he's right. And that's the root of the problem: I'm a consumer, not a trade expert. I'm more interested in finding fresh fruit than in investigating profit margins as I swoop bananas into my shopping cart. But if he is right, Europe's experience may be a warning. A *Wall Street Journal* story last year, about misleading labeling by some companies here, said that Cafe Borders adjusted its pricing after it was suggested that the company might be taking advantage of consumers' charitable instincts.

If this modern, mainstream incarnation of fair trade is under attack from the right by those who believe that free trade is the fairest trade of all, it also risks a hammering from those on the left who feel that all big business is bad business.

As Julian Baggini, who edits the British-based *Philosophers' Magazine*, put it, ethical consumerism "is characterised by three almost religious convictions: that multinationals are inherently bad; that the 'natural' and organic are inherently superior; and that science and technology are not to be trusted." So anti-globalization activists criticize huge companies such as Levi Strauss and Starbucks, even though Levi Strauss was among the first multinationals to establish a code of conduct for its manufacturing contractors and Starbucks is one of North America's largest roasters and retailers of fair trade coffee. And both can probably afford to be more altruistic than many smaller companies.

Despite efforts by nonprofits like TransFair . . . there's a lot of room for misleading labeling in our ethical shopping baskets.

These days, Starbucks should be able to harvest a steady crop of customers with a thirst for fair trade coffee. TransFair USA, the California-based FLO member that certifies imports to the United States, reported a 91 percent increase in fair trade coffee imports into the United States—from 9.8 million pounds in 2002 to 18.7 million pounds in 2003—and a 76 percent increase the following year. When I went to a D.C. Starbucks on 15th and K Streets, near my office, I did find some green packets of Fair Trade Certified coffee beans tucked away at the back of a display stand, and they didn't cost any more than the other coffee. But when I ordered a cup of fair trade coffee, I was told there wasn't any—and that I was the first customer to have requested it. Perhaps K Street isn't the best place to look for ethically aware buyers, but Starbucks itself exudes a corporate philosophy brimming with goodwill: As Chairman Howard Schultz wrote in his 2004 report, a company "can do good and do well at the same time."

At this time of the year, some people I know have taken the idea of doing good by buying well to greater heights than I ever will. Over dinner a couple of weeks ago, a friend told me what he was planning to give his adult sons this Christmas: a heifer (to be donated to a family in the developing world by Heifer International, the charity whose goal is "Ending hunger, caring for the earth") and a bag of stone-ground cornmeal (from an 18th-century Pennsylvania grist mill, which is preserved as a museum "for the pleasure and education of the public").

Unlike my friend, I'm prepared to toss a little tinsel over my conscience and spend some money for fun instead of for socially responsible reasons. Still, I did buy toothpaste from Tom's of Maine (which donates 10 percent of profits and 5 percent of paid worker time to charity). I bought stocking stuffers from the Body Shop, whose founder Anita Roddick is savvy enough to leaven her company's earnest mission statement ("To dedicate our business to the pursuit of social and environmental change") with such sprightly scents as "Zest for Satsuma" and "Perfect Passion."

And I bought handmade soap (crafted from natural oils by traditional Indian soap makers) as well as folded paper Christmas ornaments (made by a group that supports disadvantaged Bangladeshis) from a special seasonal outlet of Ten Thousand Villages, which is the company that distributes the Jakciss rugs. And I enjoyed finding out more about the artisans on the company's informative Web site.

But I'm left with a conundrum. I want to do the right thing, but I'm not prepared to make a career of it. It's not hard to find criticisms online about the Body Shop, for example; it's much harder to verify them. And I'm much less interested in checking out the story behind the bananas I buy than I am in the origin of those origami ornaments. What's more, despite efforts by nonprofits like TransFair and the International Fair Trade Association or IFAT, there's a lot of room for misleading labeling in our ethical shopping baskets. So when it comes to my food shopping in particular, I'm left wondering whether I would be doing just as much good if I simply bought the best bargain and sent the money I had saved to a development charity (as Oppenheim would have me do). Best of all might be to buy locally whenever possible, like my brother.

Even the purchase that I believe was one of my most ethical is controversial. I bought a lamb. No, not a lamb like my friend's heifer, which will help feed a family in the developing world for years to come. My lamb will feed my already well-fed family in the weeks to come. I bought it—butchered and packaged for my freezer—from my daughter's old kindergarten teacher, who lives on a farm and used to bring orphaned lambs to school to be bottle-fed.

I can't pretend that I was motivated by the need to provide the workers with a living wage, although I do know that running a profitable business helps keep property taxes down and therefore keep the farmland open. No, I bought the lamb largely because the more I've read about the lives of animals that end up shrink-wrapped on supermarket shelves, the more I've developed a distaste for mass-produced meat. So it struck me as a principled stance to know that the animal I'm eating led a happy, hormone-free life, even if it was a short one.

But try telling my vegetarian friends that. Or even the carnivorous friends who came to dinner last Sunday and could hardly stomach the fact that I had such intimate knowledge of the creature I was carving.

One man's meat, you see, can be another man's ethical predicament.

Fair Trade Labels Are Misleading

Sameh El-Shahat

Sameh El-Shahat, originally from Egypt, is a London furniture designer and sometime journalist.

There is no doubt that the concept of fair trade is an honourable and commendable one. It is after all the basis of our capitalist society. That is why we make such a big deal about transparency of stock markets to ensure "fair" prices, and that is why we come down hard on companies that collude together to fix prices.

Even best friends America and Europe sometimes get their knickers in a twist over steel import tariffs or some other issue of commercial import.

If there is one word that is treated with the same level of revulsion, by any self-respecting capitalist, as, say, child abuse, it is protectionism. That is because it goes against fair trade.

However what applies *entre nous* [between us], so to speak, is not necessarily applicable, nay even desirable, in our dealings with some of the poorer parts of the world.

Unfair Trade with the Developing World

We do not practice fair trade with the developing world. No, this is no leftist rant, just a common sense observation of the lack of either transparency or fairness in our dealings with people whom we should be encouraging to engage more in free market economics.

Talk about practicing what we preach. Take cocoa beans for example.

We are happy to remove any tariffs on African countries trying to sell them to us in the raw state, you know, straight off the tree. But god forbid that they should even think of turning themselves into chocolatiers and trying to sell us the processed beans in delectable and tasty chocolate bars. Then, they would have to endure the wrath of the EU [European Union] and the US as they impose the most punishing tariffs.

We do not practice fair trade with the developing world.

You see, the money is all in the processing of the beans and while we are happy to see pictures of grinning Africans or South Americans hand-picking ... beans for us, we have no interest in seeing similar snaps of them grinning and driving Mercedes due to a thriving chocolate-making trade. So much for fair trade.

Playing on Middle Class Guilt

Some clever clogs soon realised that discrepancy between theory and practice had created some large deposits of middle class guilt and they set about setting a fair price to it (giving fair prices to things, even ones caused by unfair situations, is one of the great pleasures of capitalism and free societies). Welcome to FAIRTRADE. It works like this.

First, you take two words, FAIR and TRADE and then you stick them together to create a brand called FAIRTRADE. Then you stick them on chocolate bars and any other kind of goods originating from a poor place (it must come from a poor place). Then you charge more for these goods to consumers who want to feel they are doing their bit to help the poor. In return the cocoa bean or banana farmers, say, receive a bit more than the market price for their produce, to give them more cash.

Fair enough. But is it really fair enough?

If FAIRTRADE goods are fairer to the poor, then why do we have to pay more for them?

How much of the extra money we pay goes to the farmers and how much to fatten the margins of big food multinationals?

Why associate helping the poor with a luxury brand that is out the reach of many in here in the West, especially with the current economic climate?

Wouldn't it be fairer if the manufacturer paid the farmers the extra bit out of their margin and still charged us the same price for the finished choccy bars?

Freer Trade Is the Key

Really fair trade would be to allow the Africans and the South Americans to make their own chocolate and pocket the processing money for themselves. Hell, they might even give our snooty and rather lazy confectioners a run for their money. Nothing better than bit of competition to add a bit of variety to the rather unoriginal selection of chocolate bars at my newsagent! I rather fancy some Ghanaian Ashanti Crunchy Surprise bars. But alas, hell will have to ice over before that happens. No, we would rather keep many countries in a state of constant underdevelopment by making sure they remain forever our suppliers of cheap raw materials.

This way they can never learn how to make chocolate, industrialise or acquire more sophisticated industries. We pay them little bit more, thanks to FAIRTRADE, to make their wretched existence more bearable, but that's about it. Having felt we have done our bit, we never really need to deal with the far meatier issues of import tariffs and trade imbalances. With our guilt satiated, we can get back to that other middle-class pastime of asking for more fairness for the Third World.

FAIRTRADE is a brand, and an excellent way for us to feel to be doing something about redressing the balance between the rich and the poor without actually doing anything of the sort.

It is long way from being FAIR TRADE. If anything, it is dangerous and misleading.

We never really know if FAIRTRADE mongers really do give the extra money that we pay to the poor the way they promise. And we are too scared to ask lest we discover something we don't want to know.

The future of capitalism depends on the world being one big free market without tariffs and without aid. Just trade.

FAIRTRADE offers, as a sweetener, to invest in the local communities of the farmers. Wouldn't it be better if we let them sell us more expensive processed goods and spend the extra money any way they want?

FAIRTRADE is therefore also condescending and reeks more of charity than of trade.

Don't let champagne socialists sell you FAIRTRADE like they sold you political correctness or multiculturalism as evidence of our being civilised. The future of capitalism depends on the world being one big free market without tariffs and without aid. Just trade.

Yes, Africa does have its fair share of banana republics for many reasons not to do with trade, but making them FAIRTRADE bananas just makes things worse, not better.

Down with tariffs, down with FAIRTRADE.

CHAPTER 2

Should Fair Trade Be Extended to Large Companies?

Chapter Overview

Zarrin T. Caldwell and Christopher Bacon

Zarrin T. Caldwell is an editor for OneWorld.net, an online media gateway for independently produced news on a host of issues that impact people worldwide. Christopher Bacon is an environmental social scientist, agroecologist, and lecturer at the Department of Environmental Studies, University of California, Santa Cruz.

While the fair trade movement has grown into a global operation with an estimated $1 billion in retail sales in 2004—and many of the small farmers and producers involved have seen marked improvements in their lives—its worldwide impact has remained small. Nonetheless, it is a growing industry and, as such, many leaders in the fair trade movement are now struggling with the way forward: how to extend the reach of the industry without selling out its founding principles of working closely with small producers to ensure they continue to reap the benefits of trade.

The Fair Trade Certification System

Much of the recent growth in the global fair trade market can be attributed to the institution of a certification system intended to clarify for consumers that, in the production of goods, certain ethical guidelines were met and producers were paid a fair price for their work. Certification was also seen as a way to grow the industry—at a time when leaders in the fair trade movement recognized that more than fifty years of solidarity-based trade had yielded profound connections, but that both sales volume and international development impacts remained limited. Thus, certification offered a way to permit wider participation and to mainstream the industry.

Debates over the certification system, however, have begun to highlight differing opinions among fair trade advocates about the future of fair trade, with some poor country producers even beginning to forgo international certification while continuing to sell through fair trade channels. Perhaps the greatest danger for producers is that all of this threatens to muddy the waters for already confused consumers—many of whom are just finding out that fair trade even exists. Additionally, the large corporations that dominate traditional global markets are now gaining increasing shares of the fair trade market—threatening to dominate the very industry that developed in opposition to their economic hegemony and raising serious questions about who is ultimately deriving the most benefit from the fair trade certification process.

The FLO certification . . . does not help consumers distinguish between companies that are entirely committed to fair trade and those that do some fair trade business.

Establishing Fair Trade Labels

Once conceptualized in the late 1980s, the initiative to certify fair trade products grew quickly—with Northern countries forming national fair trade labeling organizations and Southern producers accessing these networks. In 1997, these organizations saw the need for more uniform global standards and formed Fairtrade Labelling Organizations International (FLO). FLO has become the main worldwide body certifying that products meet fair trade principles and pledges that its process is "transparent, independent, [and] competent." Certification standards vary depending on the crop and whether the producer is a large farm or a cooperative, but they share minimum guidelines for fair treatment of producers and social and economic development. There are now some twenty national affiliates under the FLO umbrella, including TransFair USA and the Fairtrade Foundation U.K. [United Kingdom].

National divisions charge their licensees—the sellers of fair trade products—a fee for using the Fairtrade Certified label. Though initially free, producers are beginning to also pay a fee for certification, a change that has imposed an extra financial burden on many small farmers.

The expanding list of Fairtrade Certified products includes coffee, cocoa, tea, fruits, wine, sugar, honey, bananas, and rice. Coffee was among the first products certified and still accounts for a large portion of retail sales. Even for the industry's most established product, however, fair trade has only captured 1.8 percent of the U.S. coffee market and 4.1 percent of the specialty coffee market, according to TransFair USA. As low international coffee prices have inspired many farmers and roasters to seek fair trade certification, supply is currently outpacing demand, although both are growing.

The entrance of large companies into the fair trade field has sparked . . . debate.

As the fair trade industry grows, certification labels have become increasingly valuable to both companies and organizations. The FLO certification will tell a consumer whether a given product is fair trade or not, but it does not help consumers distinguish between companies that are entirely committed to fair trade and those that do some fair trade business, yet might be using the logo to imply that they are more fair-trade friendly than they are. Compare Equal Exchange, for example, which is a 100-percent fair trade coffee company, with Green Mountain Coffee Roasters, only about 20 percent of whose coffee products are fair trade.

To clarify these differences, the Fair Trade Foundation has developed a label [signifying] that 100 percent of a company's products are fair trade. Another group, the International Fair

Trade Association, certifies the organizations that advocate for fair trade and has developed its own distinct label. It sets apart mission-driven groups whose core activity is promoting fair trade from commercial businesses that have jumped into the growing industry.

Big Companies into the Fray

The entrance of large companies into the fair trade field has sparked even more debate. Where coffee is concerned, for example, companies like Starbucks, Nestlé, Proctor & Gamble, Dunkin' Donuts, and Wal-mart's Sam's Club are now all distributing fair trade lines of coffee. Some assert that this demonstrates the success of fair trade products, proving that consumers are more willing than ever to make ethical choices about their purchases. In contrast, critics argue that the FLO labeling organizations are sidling up to multinational corporations at the expense of the movement's founding principles while the corporations themselves are simply using the fair trade image for their own marketing purposes.

In September, more than 650 activists, civil society organizations, 100-percent fair trade businesses, and others tackled this and many other issues at the Fair Trade Futures Conference in Chicago. While some argued that it is critical to move ahead—even if only incrementally—with the largest corporate actors that dominate the commodities markets, others believe it has become increasingly difficult for fair trade to remain true to its original ideals. Many have questioned, for example, if empowerment of local communities—and democratic decision-making processes—can really occur when large corporations are involved. Others in the industry have pointed out that, as they hold a majority of the world's economic power, it would be a mistake to leave multinational corporations out of the equation.

Global Envision, an advocacy division of the humanitarian aid organization Mercy Corps, reported that "some sellers [at the conference] welcomed the increase in fair trade sales. They hoped to ride on the coattails of what they expect to be an expensive marketing campaign launched by corporate coffee to promote their new 'socially conscious' line. Others who consider themselves purists decided to break away from TransFair USA and a certification process they no longer believe marks an alternative to traditional trade." . . .

Some small companies, and a few big corporations, now self-certify their fair labor practices rather than going through the international certification bodies. As writer and social justice advocate Carol Estes explains in the newspaper of the Puget Consumers Co-op, "these self-certification programs can reflect serious commitment to the fair treatment of workers and sustainable growing methods, but they are open to criticism that no independent certifier is validating the claims and could be simply a marketing tool." Competing labels and claims often make the issue of fair trade that much harder for busy consumers to understand.

Greater consumer awareness about sweatshops, poor labor conditions, [and] rural poverty in developing countries . . . has led to a movement for more ethical buying choices.

Common Efforts

There is no question that the market for fair trade products is growing, but there is still not sufficient demand to meet supply and many fair trade farmers continue to sell a significant portion of their crops through conventional channels. Additionally, there is still work to do in measuring the impacts on—and ensuring the full participation of—indigenous producers, who are one of the most active—and often marginalized—subgroups within the fair trade movement. These are remaining challenges upon which many in the fair trade business can agree. But, there is good news too for fair trade advocates. Fair trade has, for example, served as a starting point for further innovations to support the farmers and growers at the beginning of the global supply chain. In addition to fair trade between the North and the South, many local, regional, and domestic initiatives have emerged to create alternative markets closer to home. In Mexico, for example, a number of business-savvy fair trade cooperative unions, certifiers, and other investors have joined together to launch Commercio Justo—the first domestic fair trade initiative in a country that primarily exports fair trade products. More such domestic initiatives may spread throughout the global South.

Educating consumers about fair trade has brought its own rewards as well, explains Laura Raynolds at the Fair Trade Research Group at Colorado State University. Raynolds asserts that the direct advocacy behind fair trade—in particular highlighting examples of programs that are working—is potentially as important in the long run as the direct benefits to those producers currently involved in the fair trade movement.

In the United States, most consumers have traditionally chosen products without taking into account where they came from, or why some are cheaper than others. Greater consumer awareness about sweatshops, poor labor conditions, rural poverty in developing countries, and unfair competition faced by small farmers has led to a movement for more ethical buying choices. Regardless of differing opinions about where the fair trade market should go, that is certainly a success story.

Fair Trade Should Not Be Dominated by Large Corporations

Wasim Salman

Wasim Salman is a senior at the University of Wisconsin-Madison, majoring in international relations.

As consumers in America, we are bombarded every day with different logos, from the Nike "Swoosh" to Microsoft's "Window." These signs are omnipresent, but there is one to which we are all exposed whether we are a part of mainstream culture or counterculture. It is a sign recognizable to anyone in Madison [Wisconsin] who drinks coffee—"Fair Trade Certified." It is present everywhere, from the bags of coffee we buy at the grocery store to our favorite coffee shop touting its own coffee as "fairly traded," but the question must be asked: Is fair trade really fair?

Fighting Exploitation

The modern fair trade movement began in 1960s Europe as a response to fears of exploitation of the Third World by large corporations. It was recognized internationally in 1968 when UNCTAD (United Nations Conference on Trade and Development) adopted it as a means to establish a fair economic (non-exploitive) relation with producers in the Third World. This led to the rise of what were called "worldshops," shops in which only fair trade products were bought and sold. These stores began to wane when it was no longer considered fashionable to buy handcrafted goods from the Third World and therefore forced organizers to rethink about how best to expand fair trade. This led to the creation of labeling initiatives in 1988. Where, before, a consumer had to go to specialty shops to purchase fairly traded goods, now the consumer would have access to fairly traded products in the stores they already purchase from.

Given this illustrious history battling exploitation and traditional business models, it is remarkable as to how horribly fair trade practices are failing producers on a global scale. First of all, fair trade creates a large amount of market inefficiency because fair trade is essentially a system of agricultural subsidies and, therefore, [it] attempts to set a price floor well above the price of the free market encouraging new producers to enter the market and already existing producers to produce more. This leads to excess in supply, which then drastically reduces the price in the non-fair trade market and costs non-fair trade farmers profits.

Corporations like Starbucks . . . have been labeled as fair-trade-certified importers even though they only import a small portion of coffee from the fair trade market.

The Evolution into an Exploitive System

This begs the question: "Why don't all farmers become fair trade certified?" The answer is simple: Because they cannot. To gain fair trade certification, a person can only be part of a co-op of small producers, leaving large coffee plantations, family plantations and lone farmers un-certifiable. Also, to become fair trade certified, one must pay roughly $2,600 for initial certification and about $650 to maintain certification each year. So not only will a producer have to find many other like-minded producers to form a co-op, but will then also be charged around $2,600 initially and roughly $650 each year merely to remain certified, while importer certification remains deceptive.

Where producer certification is limited and expensive, importer certification is broad and inexpensive. Corporations like Starbucks and Proctor & Gamble have been labeled as fair-trade-certified importers even though they import only a small portion of coffee from the fair trade market—where the amount these corporations import and the prices they pay are not public information. This loose interpretation of "fair trade certified importer" means there is no distinction between smaller importers who bring in 100 percent fair trade goods and those who bring in much, much less.

The modern state of fair trade is shameful. What began as an honest attempt to fight Third World exploitation has become an exploitive and inefficient system where, again, major corporations and First World governments rule completely. Fair trade creates extreme inefficiency and hurts anyone who is outside the fair trade market by making it ridiculously difficult and expensive to get in. To improve, this system needs to support all Third World producers, [adopt] stricter guidelines for the certification of importers and [charge] drastically reduced fees if it is to really become fair again.

The Interest of Large Companies in Fair Trade Is a Sign of Growing Ethical Consumption

Jeff Chu

Jeff Chu is a senior editor for Fast Company, *a print and online magazine that focuses on innovations in the business world.*

Global economic crisis. Financial collapse. The current climate. Whatever term you want to use to describe our present state of affairs. Funding is down, outlooks are uncertain, and people are worried. Except, perhaps, for the fair-trade folks. Demand for sustainably made, socially responsible products seems to be growing even as the global economy staggers. . . .

Candymaker Cadbury announced that, by this summer [2009], all of its flagship Dairy Milk bars in Britain and Ireland will be made exclusively from fair-trade cocoa grown by Ghanaian farmers. By the end of the year, every cup of coffee that Starbucks sells in the U.K. will be brewed with fair-trade beans, and in 2008, the company doubled the amount of fair-trade coffee it imported into the U.S. Wal-Mart is quadrupling its purchases of fair-trade bananas this year, and eliminating non-FT [fair trade] bananas from hundreds of its stores. TransFair USA is planning to certify up to a dozen new products in 2009, including avocados and olive oil, and will begin a pilot project for cotton apparel—its first beyond food. So is fair trade recession-proof?

Prices for fair-trade products may be higher, but one Harvard study has showed that consumers expect them to be:

Jeff Chu, "Are Fair-Trade Goods Recession Proof? Wal-Mart, Starbucks, and Cadbury Hope So," *Fast Company*, April 1, 2009. Republished with permission of Fast Company, conveyed through Copyright Clearance Center, Inc.

Sales actually increased when the price went up. "Not only is this consumer segment—which is growing, trend-setting—willing to pay a little more for products that speak to those values, but they expect to pay more," TransFair USA CEO Paul Rice said in a session at the forum. It's as if the higher price signals that the certification isn't just a marketing gimmick but guarantees the veracity of the claim.

Rice thinks that companies investing now are being particularly forward-looking. "Companies who are announcing big increases in FT product lines are really trying to position themselves for when we come out of the recession," he says. "They're positioning themselves now, at this unlikely moment, to establish credibility." He believes there's good reason to do so, citing studies that show up to 30% of U.S. adult consumers—some 60 million people—regularly shop for products "that are consistent with their values."

The conventional wisdom . . . seems to be that the ranks of the ethical shopper are growing.

Earlier in the week, Oxford development economist Jim Cust told me "there's arguably no altruistic act in the world. Economists look at the underlying utility you derive from doing something." That's as true of the consumer, and especially the corporation, as it is of the social entrepreneur. Fair trade is certainly seen by corporations as a differentiator for marketing purposes. "We've done something that's far beyond what any coffee company in the U.K. [United Kingdom] has ever done before," Starbucks CEO [chief executive officer] Howard Schultz said last fall. "This long-term commitment . . . will give our customers the assurance that the coffee they're buying in Starbucks in terms of espresso-based beverages is at a price that will allow sustainability for those people who need it most."

The conventional wisdom ... seems to be that the ranks of the ethical shopper are growing. The question is whether this is just what one of my acquaintances calls "an ethical corsage" thanks to clever marketing and corporate strategy, or whether the growth in fair trade really presages some kind of permanent shift in the way we consume.

Maybe fair trade seems recession-proof because the people who tend to buy those products are less vulnerable to the rises and falls of the broader economy. The one problem with the Harvard study that Paul Rice cited was that it was done at ABC Carpet & Home, an upscale Manhattan home-furnishings store/yuppie magnet frequented by folks who are a little more insulated from recession than your average consumer. They're not living paycheck to paycheck. People using food stamps aren't buying fair-trade coffee. Let's say there comes a time when smarter, fairer shopping isn't just a yuppie lifestyle choice—not the only option, but the generally preferred one. That actually could mean that fair trade becomes less recession-proof, not more.

Some Large Companies
Are Abusing Fair
Trade Certification

Rodney North

Rodney North is the owner of Equal Exchange, a natural foods co-op in Minnesota.

Something odd, and possibly very disturbing, happened recently in the United Kingdom [UK] that should interest everyone who believes that Fair Trade can help create a more just, morally grounded global economy. Nestlé—the world's largest food conglomerate, and most boycotted company—recently introduced to the UK market its first ever Fair Trade Certified product, an instant coffee called Partners Blend. But so what? Large U.S. corporations have already jumped onto the Fair Trade bandwagon. What's the problem? Don't we want corporations to move in this direction? Good point. We do. But what we're learning from the Nestlé example is that even a tiny bit of Fair Trade can go a long way to polishing even the worst corporate image, and all at the expense of real reform.

Marketplace Opportunism

For example, a recent survey in the UK, where Fair Trade enjoys a high public profile, showed that as many as 75% of otherwise knowledgeable shoppers who support Fair Trade were, in fact, mistaken and thought that the Fair Trade Certified seal meant the company had been evaluated and judged

Rodney North, "On Fair Trade 'Fig Leaves:' Equal Exchange Speaks Out on Abuse of the Fair Trade System," *Wedge.coop*, 2006. © 2006 Wedge Community Co-op, All rights reserved. Reproduced by permission.

to be free of ethical concerns. We see the same pattern in the U.S. The truth is the Fair Trade certification system examines only the individual products bearing the seal, and not companies. In the case of Nestlé it is estimated that, in fact, their Partners Blend represents less than [a] 10th of 1% of Nestlé's annual coffee imports, leaving the other 99.9% purchased the same old way. Likewise, Nestlé's vast global trade in cocoa, sugar, dairy products, and dozens of other commodities remains unchanged. So, given the "Fair Trade glow" that Partners Blend might bring to the Nestlé brand (in the UK at least), this small product launch could be a very inexpensive way to overhaul their tarnished reputation while leaving their business operations untouched.

What does this have to do with U.S. consumers? Plenty—the same rules that allow Nestlé to put on a Fair Trade figleaf in the UK market, apply in the U.S. as well. And that's why we at Equal Exchange are choosing to speak out, because we see this as the latest in a long line of actions by the world's largest food businesses to make small gestures that look good in isolation, but ultimately forestall real change for impoverished small farmers, and instead offer marketing, PR [public relations], and token efforts in its place. In the same month as Nestlé's product launch, two of the world's other largest coffee buyers also introduced Fair Trade Certified coffees, one in the U.S., and both as part of overall coffee product lines that are only 3% Fair Trade Certified, or less.

Certainly marketplace opportunism is not limited to the grocery store shelves. Examples are all around us [including] . . . non-profits who help spotlight environmental greenwashing, and firms who exploit breast cancer for marketing purposes. . . .

Conversely, Co-op America's Green Pages can help you find companies who have a more authentic commitment to responsible conduct.

Showing Corporate Sincerity

It could be argued that a corporation has to begin somewhere, and that these small product introductions at least represent a beginning—true enough. But there are signs to see if a corporation is sincere. Looking at just the realm of Fair Trade coffee—where we know something—here are some suggestions how large companies can make a convincing start:

- Convert an existing product to Fair Trade status, one that already has an established customer base.

- Offer consumers a variety of Fair Trade choices (regular, decaf, flavored, whole bean or ground, etc.).

- Utilize Fair Trade ingredients (such as cocoa, tea, sugar) in the corporation's other products.

Most importantly, convert a significant portion of coffee imports (we recommend at least 5%) to demonstrate good faith, and steadily increase that [percentage] over time. What's at risk? Corporate marketing machines making token use of Fair Trade certification can lead consumers to mistakenly associate some whole brands with Fair Trade. A false image of reform can undermine public pressure for real change. At the inception of the Fair Trade movement 20 years ago it was intended to be an alternative approach to international trade that addressed the endemic poverty, economic vulnerability, and isolation of the millions of small-scale farmers who grow most of the world's tropical agricultural commodities, and as such challenge the status quo. It was not designed as a marketing device.

Nestle's Decision to Market Fair Trade Coffee Should Be Welcomed

Mallen Baker

Mallen Baker is the editor of the Business Respect *e-mail newsletter and the development director for Business in the Community in the United Kingdom.*

Nestlé's recent membership of the Fairtrade movement should be welcomed rather than ridiculed.

Nestlé's announcement that it is to produce a "fair trade" product, supported by the Fairtrade Foundation, represents a real test of resolve for those whose stated aim is to address poverty in the supply chain.

On the one hand, some campaigners have welcomed the move (albeit rather grudgingly) for advancing the aims of Fairtrade in mainstreaming the brand and therefore making the biggest impact. Others have reacted with predictable fury, calling it the single biggest crisis to face the fair trade movement. It all depends on what we think the movement is actually for.

The true crisis is elsewhere. The global community of coffee growers is enduring real poverty and hardship as a result of the plunging prices for their product. Oversupply of coffee, exacerbated by the huge increase in production in Brazil and Vietnam, has been the principal cause. Finding solutions that alleviate this poverty must be the top priority.

Any socially responsible company operating in the coffee industry should see that it has a part to play. One company acting alone cannot solve the problem—but it can aim, along-

Mallen Baker, "Nestlé—Unfairly Roasted Over Fairtrade: Nestlé's Recent Membership of the Fairtrade Movement Should Be Welcomed Rather Than Ridiculed," Ethical Corporation, November 7, 2005. Reproduced by permission.

side governments, international bodies and development organisations to be part of the solution.

Pariah Status

Some would deny Nestlé any such role. Campaigners whose
main aim seems to be to uphold, under any circumstances, a
pariah status on the company as chief corporate villain have
been the most vocal. For instance, in response to initial reports of the Nestlé move, one development organisation said:
"The fair trade movement was set up to challenge the practices of companies like Nestlé, which have traditionally
amassed huge profits by paying their suppliers rock bottom
prices . . . How can such a company deserve the fair trade
mark?"

This is remarkable logic. We condemn this company for
paying low prices. Therefore, we want to discourage it from
taking part in a movement to pay higher prices.

---

*The campaign against poverty should welcome all willing
partners.*

Another group suggested that the real agenda was that the
company was seeking to appear ethical so it could get into
places such as student unions and church groups where it
may not currently be welcome. There remains a gulf between
non-governmental organisations and business in the understanding of what motivates business to take action in an area
such as this.

The campaigners need to decide which is more important—campaigning to alleviate poverty or campaigning against
Nestlé.

If the former, the key focus should be on the mainstream
markets first, where change has the potential to make the biggest impact. The campaign against poverty should welcome all
willing partners.

Nestle's Good Works

Nestlé has already done a considerable amount to address issues in its supply chain on coffee prices. It does more than other roasters to support greater coffee processing in the country of production, which means that more value is added in the growing country. Oxfam, in its recent report on poverty in the coffee industry, acknowledged Nestlé as standing apart in this.

The company has provided support to farmers to improve the quality and reliability of their crops—and quality brings a higher price. It also buys directly from farmers for a significant part of its intake—more than 110,000 tonnes—meaning more of the price actually goes to the farmers rather than to middlemen.

We should surely be celebrating the engagement of the most successful players in the movement for change.

This is all done for good business reasons, of course. Quality, security of supply, integrity—all these are essentials for a major corporation. It is not in its interests for farmers to go out of business.

Now, Nestlé has a Fairtrade brand. It is to be produced in accordance with the Fairtrade Foundation's standards. It is a tribute to a brand, which, according to Intel, is recognised and understood by more than 50% of consumers.

The company aims to use the product to increase the market for fair trade coffee, raising awareness still further and bringing the benefits to a wider pool of farmers. It is the most visible and controversial move within a growing trend (Kraft, for instance, has just released Kenco Sustainable Development). We should surely be celebrating the engagement of the most successful players in the movement for change.

The truth is that corporate villain Nestlé seems to be doing more to address those solutions than its critics.

Expanding Fair Trade Threatens to Reverse the Gains of the Alternative Trade Movement

Nicholas Reid

Nicholas Reid is a sales representative of the natural foods department at Equal Exchange, a fair trade store.

For years now, folks have been questioning whether the Fair Trade certifiers should have allowed plantations into a system which was founded by and for small farmer co-operatives. One of the arguments put forth to justify the entry of plantations into the system is that there are many products (such as bananas and tea) which are primarily produced by plantations and therefore are not possible to source from small farmer co-operatives. *This is a false premise.* The majority of bananas and tea ARE produced by small farmers. More importantly, by allowing plantations into the Fair Trade system, the certifiers are ensuring that products produced by small farmer co-operatives will never thrive in the Fair Trade system.

I would buy the argument that the majority of the world's tea, bananas and cocoa *for export* are grown by plantations and large-scale agriculture. But seriously, Fair Trade exists to support small farmers *because* plantations dominate banana and tea production for export. It aims to create the systems that would allow small farmers to benefit from exporting those products.

Plantations and Fair Trade

Allowing plantations into the Fair Trade system is a complete departure from the principles upon which Fair Trade was created. More importantly, it is also a betrayal of the farmers

Nicholas Reid, "Fair Trade as a Tool for Transformation: Can Plantations Play That Role?" *SmallFarmersBigChange.coop*, July 28, 2008. Reproduced by permission.

who built the system and a continuation of the marginalization of small farmers in the most impoverished countries in the world. Fair Trade was created to support organized small-scale producers and connect them to export markets. It was a response to the failure of plantation economies, and development policies designed around centralized ownership and production, to effect transformative change or economic growth that empowers and benefits people. Plantation-based Fair Trade is a slightly less gruesome extension of colonialism and slavery, and a system that for half a millennium has served only to increase global inequality.

Plantation Fair Trade does not offer a viable economic alternative to global poverty, exploitation and marginalization; it strengthens the very system that caused it. Economic history has been a stream of "slight improvements"; colonial powers invaded the "south", appropriated the land and resources, enslaved or murdered most of the population and marginalized the rest to the least productive lands. The end of political colonialism saw European plantation owners, regional despots, "princes" and "rajas", who thrived under colonialism by adopting the disastrous plantation model, quickly fill the gap of colonial magistrates.... Slavery was replaced by share-cropping and "slavery lite". Colonial interests were replaced by American and British business interests, and then transnational business interests like Chiquita and Cargill; all of whom continue to rely on the plantation model to extract resources and "produce" profits; with the added benefit of decreasing production for local consumption, making laborers more reliant on food imports; graciously provided by Cargill.

Without the Fair Trade system to provide credit and access to export markets, there is no chance a small farmer with a few acres dedicated to subsistence agriculture and a small plot of bananas could compete with Chiquita, its $4.6 billion in annual revenue, and gargantuan banana plantations. In the case of bananas, 10% of banana production is intended for export, as opposed to their starchier cousins, plantains, which are a dietary staple grown by millions of small farmers across the southern hemisphere. Bananas could be a viable and potentially lucrative and empowering market for small farmers, but allowing plantations into the Fair Trade system has marginalized small banana producers even further and ensures that they will never be successful.

Even the United States has failed to rectify the destruction of its slave/plantation economy through slight improvements. Starting with post–Emancipation Proclamation sharecropping, the advent of the "minimum wage", the civil rights movement and then affirmative action, improvements to the current labor model have not addressed, corrected or righted the destruction of the colonial-slave model. Are African-Americans better off today than they were in the early 1800s? Yes. But that leaves much—everything, in fact—to be desired: Statistics vary widely, so I won't quote them but let's just say that the number of African-American men in jail [as opposed] to college is not something this country should be proud of. The same goes for the percent of unemployed African-American men [in comparison to the percent of unemployed] white Americans. Plantation Fair Trade ignores the failures of "more fair" plantation-based economies throughout history.

Plantations, corporations and venture capital are banging on the doors of Fair Trade . . . because they see an opportunity to increase margins within their existing supply chains.

What did work in the United States was an economy based on small landholders in the Northeast and a decreased reliance on mono-crop exports. Fair Trade attempts to strengthen those economies in developing countries; to invest in small land-holders, who have the opportunity to accrue transformative assets like land and are infinitely more self-reliant through local cooperation and subsistence production. On a national level, vibrant local economies decrease dependence on foreign aid, food imports, and investment, and strengthen the ability of governments to resist egregious trade agreements and concessions.

American consumers should not be duped into supporting plantations because they agree to pay their workers a "fair wage."

Fair Wages Are Not Enough

And why, you have to wonder, are plantations and Wal-Mart so eager to join the Fair Trade system? Is it the goodness of their hearts? Or in that case wouldn't they just pay workers a fair wage because it's the right thing to do? Is it to raise their production costs through higher wages? To lower their margins for the benefit of Honduran banana farmers? Or is it that the success and hard work of small-farmer co-operatives and alternative trade organizations has led corporations and plantations to see the potential for profits in the Fair Trade system. Plantations, corporations and venture capital are banging on the doors of Fair Trade[,] begging for more quantity[;] more products[;] bigger, better, more streamlined supply-chains and relaxed regulations, because they see an opportunity to increase margins within their existing supply chains. They see people paying more for a tiny stamp on a bag of coffee; they want a piece of it. The farmers who built Fair Trade certainly don't want plantations in the system. Many consumers are confused by the debate; they trust the seal and the ideology for which it once stood.

Co-operative Fair Trade is about empowerment of people (both producers and consumers) and communities. It's about food sovereignty for people, here and in developing countries. For over twenty years, farmer cooperatives in the Fair Trade system have organized as a social and political force with which to be reckoned. Communities, tied together through economic ownership, have defined their values and developed according to their own paths of economic development. They are asserting influence and fielding politicians. Women have been empowered through shared assets and accountability, and development projects. Children are attending schools. Communities are growing their own organic food and rehabilitating the land. They are tiny green patches in the scarred and barren landscape of a scorched earth policy, vibrant local economies that value people and their connection to the earth.

Plantations, even those with labor unions and fair wages, represent continued dependence on patriarchal land-owners, predatory capital markets, transnational corporations and developed countries. American consumers should not be duped into supporting plantations because they agree to pay their workers a "fair wage", we should be investing in a viable alternative that doesn't rely on cheap labor and minority ownership. Allowing plantations into Fair Trade threatens to reverse the gains of the alternative trade movement, strengthen the competitive advantage of plantations and agribusiness, and further marginalize and exploit small farmers.

The Mainstreaming of Fair Trade Will Expand the Movement Toward Ethical Trading

Alicia Erickson

Alicia Erickson is the co-founder of twohandsworldshop.com, an online retail store that sells handmade items following fair trade practices.

Sam's Club, a division of Wal-Mart, annouced that they have converted their "private label Member's Mark premium ground coffee" to Fair Trade Certified. The process from bean begins with 3,678 small scale, independent farmers who then sell their beans to "democratically-run cooperatives for a set, guaranteed minimum price." This pool of beans from thousands of independent farmers is what composes the Member's Mark brand. In conjunction with this announcement, Sam's Club is offering a grant for teachers and students to spend one week studying the Fair Trade process of their coffee in Brazil. While this is not the first Fair Trade brand offered in either Wal-Mart or Sam's Club, it is significant as it is a bulk ground coffee targeted towards mainstream shoppers.

This new move is a mixed blessing and hits upon one of the main points of contention within the Fair Trade movement. Fair Trade has moved into mainstream and is appearing everywhere from McDonald's to Dunkin' Donuts to Wal-Mart. Any and all exposure of Fair Trade and its ideals to consumers is beneficial. And a larger market translates to more sales for producers and their communities.

Alicia Erickson, "Fair Trade Everywhere! Mainstreaming the Movement," *Green Options.com*, October 2, 2007. Reproduced by permission of the author.

Greenwashing Risks

However, as Fair Trade is embraced by large corporations with questionable ethics, so too is the potential for exploitation and weakening of Fair Trade. Similar to companies that "greenwash," to bolster their environmental credit, there are companies which seek to cash in on the feel-good PR [public relations] Fair Trade offers, without making a true commitment to the ideals and meaning of the movement. One such gap between company marketing and ethical behavior occurred when Nestle released its Fair Trade coffee in 2005. Nestle has been at the center of ethical controversy for over twenty years, with boycotts for their "aggressive and irresponsible promotion of infant formula," and for contributing to child abuse and torture within the cocoa industry, including large distribution from the Cote d'Ivoire. There was much critism of Nestle's Fair Trade coffee, and following its release, they were reported to the UK [United Kingdom] Advertising Standards Authority for a misleading and dishonest advertisement.

> "Nestlé's advertisement and website for its Fairtrade product imply it will have a significant impact on farmers in El Salvador and that the company's activities in the coffee industry are ethical. The truth is only about 200 farmers in El Salvador supply coffee for Partners' Blend [the Nestlé product] and over 3 million farmers globally who are dependent on Nestlé remain outside the Fairtrade system. Nestlé is held partly responsible for forcing down prices paid to suppliers, driving many into poverty, while its own profits have soared. Recently I interviewed a researcher from Colombia who told me 150,000 coffee farming families have lost their livelihoods due to Nestlé policies."

There is also confusion relating to the different Fair Trade labels and what they mean, and, unfortunately, companies are happy to prey upon this confusion. The Fair Trade Certified Mark means that particular product was certified. In most food products, this means it is certified at the beginning point such as farming and harvesting, but not always beyond this point. This creates opportunity for corruption at subsequent points along the way, such as with the problems with Fair Trade bananas and the exploitation of banana ripeners. Such inconsistencies occur when a company wishes to *use* Fair Trade, rather than commit to it.

Welcoming Fair Trade Expansion

Then what is the solution? Should Fair Trade be confined to its current size and guarded from the large corporate giants? I don't believe this is the solution. I believe the growth of Fair Trade, when true and committed, should be an important goal. Fair Trade is not a premium brand label, but a different approach to our entire concept of trade. The Fair Trade movement is based upon a fair and just interaction between the consumer and the producer. If the vessel for this interaction is corrupted or dishonest, then it is upon our shoulders as consumers to correct or discard the vessel for one that is more trustworthy. The fact that Fair Trade is entering large corporate retailers is not necessarily a reflection of their goodwill, and it is important to remember this. The mainstreaming of Fair Trade is, however, a reflection of our growing desire to consume ethically and responsibly and it is upon this foundation that we should build the movement and hold all participants accountable. So it is with skeptical optimism that I welcome this Fair Trade expansion, and a hope that the company will commit to the true Fair Trade and an acceptance of responsibility to ensure [it does].

Large Corporations Are Threatening Fair Trade Principles

Laura Raynolds and Douglas Murray

Laura Raynolds and Douglas Murray are co-editors, with John Wilkinson, of Fair Trade: The Challenges of Transforming Globalization.

Fair Trade has emerged in recent years as a powerful critique of conventional global inequalities and as a promising vehicle for alternative globalization grounded in social justice and ecological sustainability. It has simultaneously become a market generating $1.5 billion per year, incorporating numerous commodities and thousands of producers, consumers, and distributors in the global North and South.

Fair Trade's success is rooted in its ability to combine visionary goals with practical engagements in fair and sustainable trade within and beyond the agro-food sector. Yet its dramatic growth has fueled a number of challenges that threaten its future promise unless its vision and practice can be realigned.

In *Fair Trade: The Challenges of Transforming Globalization*, we analyze the inherent tensions of working both in, and against, the market. Is Fair Trade reshaping unequal market relations, or has its transformative agenda been eroded by the market forces it set out to change? To address this question, we investigate the impacts of Fair Trade's market success on its movement commitments around the world. As the case studies in our book demonstrate, four arenas of contestation are shaping the movement's challenges and prospects.

Laura Raynolds and Douglas Murray, "The Fair Trade Future," *Policy Innovations*, January 31, 2008. © 2008 Policy Innovations. Policy Innovations Online Magazine, a Publication of Carnegie Council for Ethics in International Affairs. www.policy innovations.org. Reproduced by permission.

Market Mainstreaming

Fair Trade has moved from the domain of small, mission-driven alternative trade organizations (ATOs) that pursue development goals into the domain of large, transnational corporations that pursue market share. Mainstreaming is made possible by the Fairtrade Labelling Organizations International (FLO) certification system and by national initiatives that promote widespread sales of certified products. This move into dominant distribution channels involves a host of large operators whose commitment to Fair Trade is open to question.

Firms that pursue a "clean washing" strategy to make their business practices seem more ethical are threatening Fair Trade principles. The case studies in our book (focusing on the role of corporate branders and retailers in American and British markets) illustrate how the certification of products controlled by large corporations may strain FLO's regulatory capacity, the integrity of standards, and the credulity of consumers. Yet they also reveal the continued importance of mission-driven ATOs and new mission-oriented firms in maintaining original movement principles.

Maintaining the small-farmer base is critical for communicating the Fair Trade concept, as well as for protecting producers.

Fair Trade products, practices, and enterprises are under constant pressure to conform to dominant market rules. Commitment to Fair Trade clearly varies, and it would be naïve to assume that corporate distributors will prioritize ethics over profits. Dedicated enterprises should receive additional support and distributor standards should be strengthened, given the power of dominant corporations to dictate supply conditions.

Plantation Production

The range of commodities, production arrangements, and enterprises involved in Fair Trade is expanding rapidly. Most notably, Fair Trade now involves a growing number of large plantation enterprises. While some argue that this expansion demonstrates the ability to transform wage labor as well as small-farmer enterprises, others assert that it fuels the integration of fundamentally unjust operations into Fair Trade networks, reinforcing North-South inequalities.

Stringent market requirements undermine the position of less-commercial farmers and cooperatives in Latin American coffee, orange juice, and quinoa production. Small-scale producers in these sectors face rising competition from more-capitalized enterprises better able to meet strict quality and quantity demands. Given the centrality to Fair Trade of direct producer-consumer links, maintaining the small-farmer base is critical for communicating the Fair Trade concept, as well as for protecting producers.

Fair Trade's fastest growth is now in large-scale enterprises, in sectors like South African horticulture and Latin American bananas. The FLO requirements for hired labor in these sectors parallel those for small farmers—with price guarantees, support for worker organizations, social premiums—and apply International Labor Organization standards. Such requirements improve labor conditions, but does Fair Trade in a plantation context go beyond other union, corporate social responsibility, and ethical trade measures? To what extent do hired laborers benefit from the price guarantees and long-term trade relations that make Fair Trade unique?

Fair Trade can be an effective strategy for supporting disadvantaged workers, but to go beyond other labor initiatives it must promote worker ownership, so that trade can be used as a vehicle for empowerment.

Network Governance

Fair Trade's internal governance challenges have increased with its growth and integration of diverse stakeholders. New Northern ATO alliances and Southern producer groups criticize the FLO certification system for under-representing producers and for advancing commercial interests over development. While recent FLO reforms have not stemmed criticism, new Fair Trade actors are moderating historical North-South divisions.

Mexican coffee farmers have spearheaded changes in FLO's Northern-led governance structure and enhanced Southern representation. Yet FLO policies and procedures—including fee structures, price levels, and top-down certification systems—remain contested. Our research finds support for concerns that Northern market priorities are guiding Fair Trade's growth, but reveals ways in which Southern interests and movement concerns are being reasserted.

Fair Trade has emerged as a key focal point of alternative globalization due to its conceptual and practical appeal.

In South Africa, for example, commercial interests have spurred the rise of new exports, yet local stakeholders have been able to link certification to development needs. In Brazil, movement groups are promoting the development of a domestic Fair Trade market as well as regional exports, counterbalancing the traditional South-to-North export model. Although local priorities often shape practices, we see the rise of a new Southern Fair Trade agenda—an agenda that reinforces the historical commitment to democratic governance, empowerment, and development.

Movement Location

The future of Fair Trade is being shaped by its engagement with larger social movements and by its location within the shifting boundaries of state, economy, and civil society. Fair Trade has traditionally been defined by the competing visions of the more market-oriented and ascendant FLO certification system and the more movement-oriented and less dynamic ATO sector. Yet these two wings are creating common ground via joint advocacy and increased engagement with broader trade equity and sustainability movements.

In the global North, these efforts bolster Fair Trade's political agenda and the conscientious consumerism that underpins sales. In the global South, Fair Trade is positioned at the nexus of agrarian reform, food sovereignty, cooperative, and solidarity economy movements. It is being drawn into central policy arenas and is tied directly to government programs in countries like Brazil and South Africa.

Fair Trade has emerged as a key focal point of alternative globalization due to its conceptual and practical appeal. It captures the complex local/global and social/ecological concerns of the movement, and provides a guide for translating trade justice ideas into practice.

Realigning Vision and Practice

A new wave of Fair Trade is starting to swell. Tensions persist between the movement's traditional goals of transforming conventional trade and its market goals of promoting more egalitarian commodity chains. Yet, the recent focus on expanding Fair Trade markets may be reaching its limits. The next wave rejects the notion that market growth should be seen as an unqualified sign of success.

Producers, consumers, and alternative trade organizations around the world are reasserting Fair Trade's development priorities. And FLO and its national initiatives have started to rekindle political commitments and build alliances. As our book concludes, Fair Trade is realigning its vision and practice to continue the task of transforming globalization.

CHAPTER 3

Is Fair Trade Compatible with Free Trade?

Chapter Overview

Daniel W. Drezner

Daniel W. Drezner is associate professor of international politics at the Fletcher School at Tufts University. This essay is extracted from U.S. Trade Strategy: Free Versus Fair, *published by the Council on Foreign Relations.*

Trade is vital to the U.S. economy. In 1970, the sum of imports and exports was less than 12 percent of gross domestic product. By 2004, that figure had doubled to 24 percent. U.S. exports accounted for approximately 25 percent of economic growth during the 1990s, supporting an estimated 12 million jobs. From agriculture to manufacturing to technology to services, the U.S. economy needs international trade to prosper.

Despite trader's importance to America, U.S. trade policy seems like it is at a standstill. Both the Doha [the capital of Qatar] round of world trade talks and negotiation over the proposed Free Trade Area of the Americas are deadlocked. The legislative branch is putting enormous pressure on the [executive branch] to punish China for its large bilateral trade surplus. . . .

Negative Attitudes About Free Trade

Why has U.S. trade policy ground to a halt? Shifts in domestic attitudes and world politics have combined to create one of the least hospitable environments for trade liberalization in recent memory. The most dramatic shift in opinion came from Americans making more than $100,000 a year. According to the Program on International Policy Attitudes (PIPA), support in that income group for promoting trade dropped to 28 percent in 2004 from 57 percent in 1999. A September

2005 German Marshall Fund (GMFUS) survey revealed that 57 percent believe that freer trade destroys more American jobs than it creates, and 58 percent of Americans would favor raising tariffs for imported goods if it meant protecting jobs—a higher number than in Germany, France, or Great Britain. Healthy majorities believe that trade primarily benefits multinational corporations at the expense of small businesses.

Three political facts of life have caused many Americans to shift their support from free trade to fair trade. First, during times of economic uncertainty, public suspicion of free trade policies explodes into public hostility. Inevitably, foreign trade becomes the scapegoat for business-cycle fluctuations that have little to do with trade. Second, it is particularly difficult to make the case for trade expansion during election years. Trade generates diffuse benefits at concentrated costs. Those who bear the costs are more likely to vote on the issue—and make campaign contributions based on the issue—than those who reap the benefits. Third, both advocates and opponents simultaneously inflate the importance of trade while framing the issue as a zero-sum game. Trade is both blamed and praised for America's various economic strengths and ills, even though domestic factors—such as macroeconomic policy, fluctuations in the stock market, and the pace of innovation—matter more for America's economic performance.

U.S. trade policy is at a crossroads between pursuing freer trade or fairer trade.

At the same time, the WTO [World Trade Organization, an international body that regulates world trade] has become a victim of its own success. Over the past forty years each successive round of GATT [General Agreement on Tariffs and Trade]/WTO trade talks has taken longer to complete. The Uruguay round took seven years from start to finish; during that time, NAFTA [North Atlantic Free Trade Agreement], was proposed, negotiated, and ratified. In the Doha round, China, India, and Brazil have created their own negotiating bloc, and African countries have exercised their voice as well. Some of these new players helped to sabotage the Cancun ministerial meeting in the fall of 2003. The larger developing countries have much greater market power than they did thirty years ago, and these economies all have dramatically higher growth rates than the United States, making it impossible to ignore their negotiating positions. It is simply much harder to reach a consensus with more than 150 countries participating in the process.

Free trade is less difficult to negotiate but more difficult to sell at home, while fair trade is more difficult to negotiate but less difficult to sell at home.

Free Trade or Fair Trade

U.S. trade policy is at a crossroads between pursuing freer trade or fairer trade. A free trade approach would jumpstart Doha by cutting agricultural subsidies or allowing greater crossborder movement of foreign workers; pursuing free trade agreements with South Korea, India, or Japan if the Doha round cannot be restarted, and pledging an all-out political push for the renewal of TPA [Trade Promotion Authority, the authority for the U.S. president to negotiate trade agreement that Congress cannot amend or filibuster] in early 2007. A fair trade approach would refuse to make further concessions in the Doha round of negotiations until developing countries and the European Union demonstrate a greater receptivity to American exports; halting bilateral free trade agreements with developing countries; and relying more on "managed trade" arrangements, unilateral trade sanctions, escape clauses and safeguard mechanisms to rebalance U.S. trade.

The free trade orientation provides a more coherent set of economic policies, but carries a significant political risk. Adopting a free trade orientation will promote economic growth, control inflation, and reaffirm U.S. economic leadership to the rest of the world. At the current moment, however, freer trade runs against the tide of public and congressional opinion—the political price of this policy will be steep. The fair trade orientation provides a more popular set of policies, but carries a significant policy risk. Adopting a tough position on slowing down imports while boosting exports will resonate strongly with many Americans. Because almost any trade barrier can be advocated on grounds of fairness to some group, however, special interests can easily hijack this policy orientation. Internationally, such a policy will be viewed as an abdication of U.S. economic leadership. Slowing down imports will encourage other countries to erect higher trade barriers against U.S. exports. Any kind of global trade war would severely damage the American economy—and American workers.

Free trade is less difficult to negotiate but more difficult to sell at home, while fair trade is more difficult to negotiate but less difficult to sell at home. Because of the current political climate, the choice faced by [the U.S. President] . . . and [the president's] advisors is a daunting one.

Fair Trade and Free Trade Are Two Sides of the Same Coin

Phil Goff

Phil Goff is currently the leader of the New Zealand Labour Party. Between 1999 and 2008 he served in a number of government positions, including minister of defense, minister of corrections, minister of foreign affairs and trade, minister for disarmament and arms control, and associate minister of finance.

I've been asked to speak to you about New Zealand's role as a responsible global citizen in relation to free vs fair trade.

'Free trade' and 'fair trade' can mean different things to different people.

To some, the two are seen as incompatible.

Some associate the term free trade with big business, the opening of new markets and securing better returns on more exports.

Fair trade, on the other hand, is often seen as being about looking after the individual—for example making sure producers in the developing world are properly paid for their goods or labour.

Both these views have some merit. Freer trade does lead to increased trade flows and greater prosperity, for individuals as well as business.

Trade is fair when it is allowed to take place in an open, non-discriminatory global trading system, based on predictable and equitable rules.

And 'fair trade' initiatives are also useful in helping developing country producers escape the cycle of poverty.

Phil Goff, "Fair Trade and Free Trade—Two Sides of the Same Coin," *Beehive.govt.nz*, July 5, 2008. Reproduced by permission.

However, I would disagree with the assertion that free trade and fair trade are incompatible. They are in fact two sides of the same coin, and both are important aspects of New Zealand's role as a responsible global citizen.

Trade and Developing Nations

The New Zealand Government is of the view that trade is fair when it is allowed to take place in an open, non-discriminatory global trading system, based on predictable and equitable rules.

It is a fact that trade can lift people out of poverty, and that more trade lifts more people out of poverty. We need look no further for an example of this than China, where free market policies instituted by the Chinese Government have lifted over 500 million people out of poverty.

Oxfam International [a nongovernmental organization that fights global poverty] estimates that if developing countries could increase their share of world exports by just 5 percent this would generate some US$350 billion in additional income—much larger than any aid package.

More trade in an open, rules-based trading system gives poorer countries more money to tackle poverty. It also leads to increased interaction within the global system and greater access to technologies and skills.

Poor countries rightly blame subsidies and other trade barriers in the developed world as denying them the opportunity to earn a living in the global marketplace.

Kofi Annan, [former] Secretary General of the United Nations, said that no single change could make a greater contribution to eliminating poverty than by fully opening the markets of prosperous countries to the goods produced by poor ones.

The current round of WTO [World Trade Organization, an international body that regulates world trade] negotiations was christened the Doha Development Agenda [launched in

2001 and still in negotiations, the Agenda seeks to lower trade barriers around the world]. This reflects the fact that development is its central goal.

The WTO recognises the significant degree of inequality that exists among its members. Therefore, while looking to open up markets and improve access, the Doha Round also provides for what is known as 'special and differential treatment' for developing countries.

This means, for example, that developing countries may be allowed to make lesser tariff cuts, or be subject to longer implementation periods for their WTO trade commitments, than their developing country counterparts.

In addition, mechanisms to safeguard at-risk producers in developing countries in times of crisis may be agreed.

For the poorest, the so-called 'least developed' countries, even greater flexibility is provided.

One of the most important trade and development outcomes from the Doha Round would be reform of agriculture trade. Seventy percent of the world's poor are involved in agriculture.

The reduction of farm subsidies, tariffs and other barriers to agricultural trade will enable developing countries to secure enhanced access to large new markets, and to enjoy the benefits of fair prices for their products in these markets.

If we can achieve this, then we are achieving 'fair' trade on a global scale.

Ensuring Freedom of Trade

New Zealand is committed to an ambitious result in the Doha Round—including in agriculture. Such an outcome will [be beneficial not only] to New Zealand.

Developing country agricultural producers stand to gain significantly through greater market access for their products, particularly into developed countries, many of which continue to protect their producers through subsidies and other trade barriers.

We don't just talk the talk. As a country, we consistently rank as having amongst the lowest levels of market barriers in the world.

We have allowed Least Developed Countries to export their goods to New Zealand completely free of any tariffs or quotas since 2001.

And we support initiatives for special and differential treatment for developing countries in the WTO—in particular appropriately tailored provisions that give developing countries additional flexibilities for food and livelihood security, and rural development.

The Doha negotiations are more than just about getting a good deal. They are also about creating certainty and rules in trade. We need robust international governance in trade as much as we do in the environment, human rights and security.

Global trade rules limit the scope for discrimination and provide certainty for traders. The WTO also provides the means for redress through dispute settlement procedures when global trade rules are broken. For smaller, or less wealthy or powerful members of the international trading systems these rules are crucial.

Growing concerns about food security, the so-called 'global credit crunch' and higher commodity and fuel prices make it even more important that the international community work together to remove global trade distortions.

According to the United Nations' Food and Agriculture Organisation, world food prices rose 40 percent last year and already this year by a further 50 percent. This is a problem for all of us. For increasing numbers it is a crisis.

For poor households in developing countries, the consequences of food inflation are not just pressure on family budgets but malnutrition and hunger. Increasing food prices mean that another 100 million people will be pushed into poverty.

In response to these challenges it is crucial that we assert even more strongly the need for a robust rules-based multilateral trading system. To do this, we need to redouble efforts towards a successful conclusion to the Doha Development Round.

Support to help developing countries maximise their gains from trade is . . . an important complement to reforming the rules of trade.

Ensuring the freedom of trade does not, by itself, ensure the fairness of trade. It is merely one side of the coin.

Ensuring Fairness of Trade

Many developing countries face real challenges in taking advantage of the opportunities that emerge as trade barriers fall.

They may have limited resources, poor institutional capacity, small productive sectors, and lack critical social and economic infrastructure.

Support to help developing countries maximise their gains from trade is therefore an important complement to reforming the rules of trade. Last year New Zealand provided $28.8 million of assistance in Aid for Trade and an additional $9 million for infrastructure projects, such as building roads.

We are also an active voice in international discussions to ensure the effectiveness of Aid for Trade.

The government has also provided support through its international development agency, NZAID [New Zealand's International Aid and Development Agency], to build consumer awareness in New Zealand of the availability of fair-trade-accredited products.

New Zealand and Australia are currently among the fastest-growing markets in fair trade goods of any countries in the world.

We are a country that depends on trade for its well-being, and I think that while most New Zealanders accept that enhanced access for our goods into new markets is critical to our continued economic growth and prosperity, we also believe that—fundamentally—such arrangements should also be fair.

This is reflected in the approach the government takes to our bilateral trade deals. In these agreements we do not neglect our commitment to principled trade.

We seek to integrate labour and environmental standards into our trade agreements because we believe that while developing countries should not be denied the legitimate comparative advantage of lower costs, this advantage should not be secured in return for neglecting fundamental labour or environmental principles.

Earlier this year [2008], New Zealand celebrated the historic achievement of becoming the first developed country to sign a free trade agreement with China.

The agreement is comprehensive, including goods and services but also chapters on investment, labour and the environment, as well as provisions relating to the Treaty of Waitangi [New Zealand's founding document].

The inclusion of labour and environment provisions is an important condition of all New Zealand's free trade agreements. Often, this can make it hard to get a deal as some countries are reluctant to include such provisions in what they view as essentially trade agreements.

In the case of China, however, we became the first country to negotiate binding labour and environment outcomes as part of our FTA [free trade agreement] package.

In the end, it is our consistent and principled approach to trade which ensures we are respected by our trading partners.

We believe, advocate for and practice trade that is both free and fair. We recognise that they are two sides of the same coin. And we put our money where our mouth is.

Fairer Trade Is the Middle Ground Between Protectionism and a Completely Free Market

Devin T. Stewart

Devin T. Stewart is director of the Global Policy Innovations program at the Carnegie Council for Ethics in International Affairs, an organization that promotes ethics in international affairs.

Globalization is again under attack. Commentators from many perspectives have argued recently that globalization has reached a turning point and will never recover. Global inequities, failures of international institutions, and resentment of American power, they say, will usher in worldwide protectionism, threatening to end the current era of globalization.

An end to the current state of globalization doesn't have to lead to conflict, however, as did the pre-1914 era. Indeed, Washington's new political makeup provides an opportunity to shape a globalization that benefits all. In the realm of international trade, a starting point may be to reconcile free and fair trade.

A new, fairer U.S. trade policy would aim to give more people the opportunity to enjoy the benefits from world trade flows.

Free Versus Fair Trade

After all, while the freest economies tend to be the richest, trade isn't an end in itself. Rather it is a tool to help increase

Devin T. Stewart, "United States Must Redefine 'Fair Trade,'" *Policy Innovations*, January 29, 2007. Policy Innovations Online Magazine, a Publication of Carnegie Council for Ethics in International Affairs. www.policyinnovations.org. Reproduced by permission.

living standards, lower poverty, and advance political freedom and human rights. U.S. Congressman Sandy Levin, the new trade subcommittee chairman, recently issued a statement to this effect, adding that the terms of international competition must be shaped to achieve both growth and equity.

The concept of freedom seems pretty straightforward, but fairness means different things to different people. Fair trade is often depicted as antithetical to free trade, or as protectionism in disguise. Nevertheless, freedom and fairness are decent principles to guide an ethical U.S. economic policy, and reconciling the two would help restore American moral leadership. Fairness in economics is often concerned with offsetting "unfair" advantages created by lower wages in trading partners, but this notion incorrectly views the global economy as a zero-sum game.

A new, fairer U.S. trade policy would aim to give more people the opportunity to enjoy the benefits from world trade flows. Although Congress may attempt to use the term fairness to protect vulnerable domestic industries, doing so would be a mistake. As [former] Treasury Secretary Henry Paulson recently said: "Giving in to protectionist sentiment would send a terrible signal. We would be telling developing nations that while we have benefited from increased trade, we aren't going to allow them the same opportunity to develop." He concluded that such a direction would be "morally wrong."

[Scottish philosopher] Adam Smith showed that economic freedom allows people to maximize their potential to the benefit of all society. But total freedom, as [British philosopher] Thomas Hobbes argued, leads to a short and nasty life. The Aristotelian notion of moderation might help reconcile this paradox: Trade should be neither too free nor too regulated.

This is the puzzle a group of philosophers, economists, and practitioners tackled last month [December 2006] at the Carnegie Council. The question posed was, is it possible to fashion a free and fair trade policy that will build a more sustainable and equitable trading system? And, how can the principles of a more moral trade policy be applied to extractive industries? Three "freedoms" are worth examining here.

Freedom to Trade Anything

As philosopher Christian Barry has noted, some goods are unfit for trade. For example, it is widely maintained that some services, such as those offered by an assassin, should not be traded. Goods obtained through coercion may also be deemed unfit for trade. When it comes to the trade in natural resources, it is not always clear that the sellers are the rightful owners of the goods, as they may have obtained them through bullying.

The issue of rightful ownership pertains also to trade in intellectual property. One question under debate is how to protect cultural intellectual property. For example, Ghana imports traditional African textile prints from China. Exacerbating tensions over Chinese textiles in Africa and the resulting loss of African jobs, some scholars have begun to question the fairness of trade in another country's cultural goods. The answer may lie in determining whether these vendors are the rightful owners of this property.

As the greatest beneficiary of globalization, the United States has a responsibility to give back to the system from which it benefits.

The process of producing goods traded should respect human rights and a country's labor and environmental laws. Slavery, poor working conditions, and environmental degradation are particularly problematic in illegal mining and logging operations. As a result, multinational corporations have started carefully scrutinizing their supply chains. Ford Motor and General Motors, for example, recently stopped using Latin American pig iron produced by slave labor. DaimlerChrysler,

Ford, GM, and Honda joined together last month to train suppliers to avoid buying materials made by slaves.

Freedom to Trade with Anyone

Makers of a decent trade policy should remember the premise that trade is meant to improve people's lives, and they should deliberate when considering the use of trade barriers, sanctions, and embargos. The record shows that these tools are blunt and inaccurate in achieving broad security goals. Policy toward North Korea, for example, is often thought to be a choice between advancing human rights or a proliferation regime—or both. Instead, we have witnessed nuclear proliferation and mass famine on the Korean Peninsula despite a politically gratifying U.S. trade embargo.

The other side of the coin concerns trading partners that fail to enforce their own labor, human rights, and environmental standards, jeopardizing another kind of security. Part of the problem is simply keeping tabs on corporate behavior and publicizing the findings. [Nongovernmental organizations] Oxfam and the Business and Human Rights Resource Centre have excelled in this area. A country's human rights record may matter little if the trading partner feels that the exported good, for example oil, is vital to its national security. The United States must do its part to lower oil demand and invest in renewable energies, helping oil-exporting nations to shed the resource curse.

Freedom to Trade with Impunity

As the greatest beneficiary of globalization, the United States has a responsibility to give back to the system from which it benefits. In practical terms, this means the United States has an interest in working toward nurturing freedom and fairness not only at home but also in the global economy. It can do so by promoting fair and ethical trade practices, socially responsible business models, expanded stakeholder rights, and a stronger global civil society. The responsibility is great but fair for the biggest consumer of the world's resources.

These limits on free action can guide a fairer trade policy. Constructive policies are available to implement that vision. The U.S. Congress has made a promising start by passing bills to raise the minimum wage, make higher education more affordable, and eliminate subsidies for the U.S. oil industry, shifting resources toward developing clean energy technologies. It is also hopeful that Max Baucus, the . . . chairman of the Senate Finance Committee, would like to renew the Trade Adjustment Assistance program [which gives the U.S. president fast-track trade negotiating authority]. He also supports a broader "Global Adjustment Assistance" that would offer benefits to workers displaced not just by trade, but by all aspects of globalization.

Enacting Fair Trade

To combat protectionist temptation and build on the ability of the country to cope with the tides of globalization, U.S. trade policy should also tailor its primary and secondary education system to equip graduates with the skills to compete in a global economy by emphasizing science, engineering, and foreign languages. The United States will be forced to take a look at redirecting resources away from war and toward upgrading its own infrastructure. New York City's status as the preeminent financial center is threatened by cities like London and Tokyo.

To realize Baucus's goal of renewing fast track trade negotiation authority, the U.S. Congress must feel it has the capital to support trade agreements, otherwise fast track will be stuck in a pit stop. "Fair trade" agreements or comprehensive economic partnership agreements would continue the tradition of including labor and environmental provisions, like those with Jordan and Chile. A Washington trade journalist recently put it to me: "Labor and environmental enforcement is needed so that politicians feel comfortable enough to support FTAs [free trade agreements] without getting clobbered by labor groups. Then we can renew fast track."

These comprehensive agreements commit partners to enforce their own environmental and labor laws, which in turn comply with the International Labor Organization. They could also offer deeper integration in the areas of labor movement and port screening, for example, to trading partners that honor the freedoms of speech, assembly, and religion. These three freedoms are good proxies for transparency, labor rights, and civil society, all necessary for the establishment of fair trade practices.

Other powerful approaches include fair trade and ethical trade initiatives. As clean energy consultant David Dell puts it: That which is truly profitable is also sustainable and that which is truly sustainable is profitable. Social entrepreneurs, local governments, and increasingly business gurus like Michael Porter have reached this axiom. To these ends, fair trade initiatives, such as Hand Crafting Justice and Global Goods Partners, seek to cut out the middleman, pay producers fair wages, and reinvest in community health and education.

[Trade] openness—with the proper safety net—can help advance human rights.

Ethically traded goods are those produced by companies that ensure labor standards are enforced within their own company and by their suppliers. Another idea is for companies to shoulder some of the burden of providing a safety net to those laid off when jobs are moved to take advantage of cheaper labor. Trade adjustment insurance and freer labor flows are part of the compact of free trade that is yet unfulfilled.

Freedom and Justice for All

The above initiatives define corporate social responsibility: philanthropy and reinvestment, good labor practices, and business models that benefit people and the planet as a whole. They help sustain a healthy trading system and act as a de facto "trade Peace Corps," putting a human face to an American-led free market system. Given the services these initiatives provide to American leadership, the U.S. government should consider bolstering them by establishing a fund to support grassroots fair trade activities and giving tax breaks to socially responsible business models.

Notice that tariffs and competitive devaluations are not on the list. Although both of these approaches are advocated under the guise of protecting fairness and even human rights, history and economics tend to dispute those claims. Instead, openness—with the proper safety net—can help advance human rights.

For the United States to justify and prolong its international leadership, it must ensure that the rest of the world can access the benefits of globalization. It can start by promulgating a more thoughtful approach to trade—one that is neither protectionist nor free market fundamentalist. By finding a middle road between these extremes, the United States can realize its own dream of freedom and justice for all.

Fair Trade Policies Go Beyond Free Trade to Promote Long-Term Global Economic Growth

Bama Athreva

Bama Athreva, a cultural anthropologist, is the executive director of the International Labor Rights Forum, a nonprofit advocacy organization dedicated to achieving just and humane treatment for workers worldwide.

Notwithstanding the media outcry from corporate America, reports of the demise of free trade are a bit premature. It is true that a stimulus package of $819 billion was approved Wednesday, January 28 [2009] by the House of Representatives and is likely to win Senate passage this week [the economic stimulus package was signed into law February 17, 2009], and that this package included "Buy America" procurement provisions. It is unlikely in the extreme, though, that these provisions will, as critics have claimed, spark a global trade war. Rather than wasting its political capital fighting "Buy America," corporations might better serve their long-term interests by promoting parallel initiatives to stimulate growth and good jobs in emerging markets.

The Critics' Complaints

The US Chamber of Commerce, spearheading the offensive, has stated that the procurement provisions in the stimulus package would "trigger retaliation from our trading partners." It bears noting that the Chamber has expressed "concerns" with elements of the package beyond the Buy America clauses. . . .

Bama Athreva, "Protecting U.S. Workers Without 'Protectionism,'" *ConnectUSFund.org*, February 4, 2009. Copyright 2009 The Connect U.S. Fund. Reproduced by permission.

Be that as it may, let's deal with the "straw man." A trade war among developed nations, or between developed and developing nations, would be a devastating turn of events as nations struggle to deal with the impacts of what is a global economic crisis. However, it is unlikely in the extreme that any nation would be the first to "go nuclear" [declare trade war] in this sense. The US business community knows this. Others have made the point elsewhere so I'll simply reference the fact that "Buy America" procurement criteria have been around for a long time and haven't succeeded in sparking a trade war yet, and that the reasons ... are that such criteria are arguably fully compliant with the WTO [World Trade Organization, an international body that regulates world trade] agreement on government procurement.

The UK [United Kingdom] and France are struggling to make peace with their own domestic labor movements' demonstrations over unpopular policies. China, which is facing its own very serious unemployment crisis, with literally millions of angry and laid off workers, announced as early as November 2008 its own comprehensive domestic stimulus package, with major new investments in housing, rural infrastructure, health and education and the Chinese government has recently offered $10 billion in subsidies to its domestic textile industry. Interpreting such policy responses through the narrow lens of free trade does an injustice to the broader cause free trade is intended to serve: global stability and prosperity. This may be a time to deviate from the free trade path to achieve that larger goal.

Pro-Worker Policies Internationally

Beyond the smoke and mirrors, the real issue is that millions of workers around the world are losing their jobs, and developing country workers in export sectors reliant on the US market have been particularly hard hit. What can policymakers do to enact policies that benefit workers around the world, and in particular in developing countries, and not just American workers?

> Trying to find ways to lower [production] costs even further—a "race to the bottom"—will not drive long-term global economic growth.

For many years, US trade and development policies, enacted through legislation such as the Africa Growth and Opportunity Act, have been promised on the presumption that the best strategy for growth for LDCs [less developed countries] was to hitch their wagons to . . . US consumer demand. This is a moment to re-think the conventional wisdom, and consider sensible alternatives that respond to the real current crisis. Workers around the world are losing jobs by the millions because of a massive global economic recession and a huge downturn in US consumer spending. Champions of free trade would do well to revisit [the] old prescription that poor countries wed their economic hopes to the US consumer market; surely there are other possibilities to create sustainable and decent employment in the current global context.

> The crisis may provide a policy opportunity to get beyond "free trade" and into what advocates have been calling "fair trade" for many years.

Beyond "sweatshop" jobs, can we help create decent and sustainable jobs that raise workers into the middle class? This would be a win-win for US companies; retailers and companies reliant on global sales are hurting because sales are down. As US consumer growth in recent years has relied on ever lower prices for consumer goods, such companies are worried about keeping costs of production down—hence the fear of a trade war. Trying to find ways to lower costs even further—a "race to the bottom"—will not drive long-term global economic growth. Given the current crisis, a better approach would be to raise real wages and lower unemployment in US, so that the US consumer can buy more.

Even more forward-thinking would be promoting policies that increase prosperity in the "emerging markets" of interest to many of these global corporations. Prosperous, stable middle classes in India, China, Mexico and Indonesia are critical to future global prosperity and stability—as well as support for open markets. Yet, real wages in light manufacturing in these countries have stagnated in recent years. We need to re-think what kinds of trade and development policies are needed to ensure that job growth in these countries measures not only quantity but quality of jobs—are the jobs created unstable and low-wage, or do they represent decent and sustainable employment—the kind that ultimately lets workers rise into the middle classes?

US trade and investment policies should integrate investor protections and benefits with requirements to create stable and decent employment.

More Fair Trade Needed

The crisis may provide a policy opportunity to get beyond "free trade" and into what advocates have been calling "fair trade" for many years—trade that benefits not only investors, but importantly, the producers of wealth—the people [who] grow the commodities and assemble the products that are traded. "Fair trade" does require protections, but is not protectionist. The conditions of trade require that investors seeking the benefits of production in the developing world, including comparatively lower wages, agree to a floor of decent working conditions that ultimately enable workers to lift themselves out of poverty.

Labor and trade linkage is nothing new, but it needs to be expanded. While labor and trade linkage has had some success, most notably in Cambodia, it has failed to address significant development challenges that go beyond core labor right—in particular, the need for stability of employment. This conditionality also fails to provide protection for global supply chain workers who do not fit our conventional understanding of labor, most notably, the contract and farm labor prevalent in global agricultural production.

Investors worldwide benefit from the ability to move production not only in manufactured goods but in agricultural products to low-wage developing countries. . . . [P]ermanent employment has become less prevalent in light manufacturing, [however,] and practically nonexistent in global commercial agriculture. US trade and investment policies should integrate investor protections and benefits with requirements to create stable and decent employment in relevant sectors. This would help to shelter workers from shocks in times of global downturn, and would enable them to make gains in good times that would ultimately help to sustain and grow global consumer markets.

US corporations worried about global backlash should take a look at what they themselves can do to ensure that private investment contributes to sustainable development. Are investors willing to direct investments to countries and regions where there is relatively better enforcement of labor laws? Are they willing to make long-term commitments to suppliers? Are they willing to publicly support domestic initiatives to strengthen labor protections, protections for farmers (in areas such as land rights or stronger commodity policy), or overall social safety nets? Are they willing to be transparent about both their supply chains and revenue flows? This is in their long-term interests as it will raise purchasing power of consumers in developing countries, promote strengthened rule of law, and help to grow the emerging markets that will be of great significance in a changing global economic order.

Global Development Can Come Only Through Free Trade, Not Fair Trade

Janet Daley

Janet Daley is a political commentator for The Telegraph, *a British newspaper.*

As you glide along the supermarket aisle past the smartly packaged Fairtrade coffee and guiltily slip the cheaper arabica [coffee] into your trolley [shopping cart] instead, you may ask yourself how much good your overpriced purchase of the Fairtrade stuff would have done anyway.

Well, now you know. Today's [January 1, 2009] report from the Adam Smith Institute will probably confirm your suspicion: Fairtrade labelling is largely a marketing ploy, which makes clever use of the almost infinite capacity for guilt harboured by the residents of wealthy countries over the condition of those in poorer ones, even though that condition is, in no rational sense, their fault.

> *By sustaining agricultural activity that would not otherwise be sustainable in the global marketplace, [Fairtrade] keeps backward populations from developing.*

But rational thinking does not come into this: you and your heaped shopping trolley represent wealth and security, which you have a vague but pretty firm notion that the people who harvest the coffee beans do not have. So maybe you are persuaded to make a gesture: a small strike against "exploitation" and global greed and "corporate capitalism". And you feel better about yourself.

It transpires that a very small number of farmers are getting a subsidised fixed price for their produce under Fairtrade franchises and that this is at the expense of most other farmers in their regions, who are actually worse off as a result.

> *What developing countries need is to develop, not to have their present conditions of life and work preserved like a museum exhibit.*

Real Development Needed

But even more serious, the Fairtrade operation helps to keep poor countries and undeveloped economies exactly that—poor and undeveloped.

By sustaining agricultural activity that would not otherwise be sustainable in the global marketplace, [Fairtrade] keeps backward populations from developing other forms of modern economic activity that might help them climb out of their backwardness. In order to permit wealthy people to indulge in a bit of sentimental largesse, it effectively preserves an anachronism that locks some of the poorest people in the world in backwaters of primitive economic existence.

What developing countries need is to develop, not to have their present conditions of life and work preserved like a museum exhibit. And the greatest aid to real development—and the proven route out of mass poverty—is through free trade, not Fairtrade.

The Meaning of "Fair"

All of which should cause us to reflect on the various misuses of the word "fair", and its even more pernicious noun form "fairness", as it is bandied about in political discourse. As received opinion has it, "fair" means "equal"—in the strict literal sense of the word. Distribution of wealth in a society is "fair" if nobody has much more than anybody else—however much harder they may have worked, or however singular and disciplined their talents may be.

The corollary of this is that taxation helps to ensure "fairness" by seeing to it that those who earn more than others have more of their income confiscated. On this formulation, disparities of wealth are inherently wicked. This is a moral philosophy that you may or may not find attractive. But if you do, you will have to accept that it is fundamentally totalitarian. Disparities of wealth are a sign of a dynamic free-market economy in which some sectors are invariably expanding while others contract: at any given moment, some people's lot will be improving ahead of others'.

The more robust and dynamic the economy is, the more dramatic these spurts of certain sections of the economy will be. That is why disparities of wealth became more "unfair" during the [Prime Minister Margaret] Thatcher revolution in the 1980s—because the [United Kingdom] economy was waking up from its moribund state and leaping about all over the place.

The Left-liberal remedy for these disparities of wealth— enforced "fairness" by redistribution and heavy regulation of the economy—must penalise, or at least discourage, precisely those activities that are the most energetic, innovative and productive of wealth.

But the Fairtrade business should indicate that there is a quite different way of approaching this: instead of artificially subsidising poverty and lack of initiative by redistributing the wealth of the hard-working, a society could define "fairness" as creating more opportunity for self-determination in a vibrant free economy that encourages change, flexibility and personal development.

In other words, it could stop protecting people from any possible risk or consequence of failure and instead allow the economy to create as many new ventures and avenues as the market can bear, with all the myriad openings for idiosyncratic talents and temperaments that would create.

It is ironic that the very same people who are committed to the idea that "fair" must mean "the same" talk endlessly about "opportunity". Nothing is a greater killer of opportunities than uniformity.

Conversely, school selection is "unfair" if able children and conscientious parents are more likely to gain entry to "good" schools (which are only as good as they are because those children and their parents choose to go to them). So for educational opportunity to be fairly distributed, children must be allocated to schools by a blind lottery that takes no account of their abilities, their temperaments, their inclinations or their compatibility with the school's attitudes. This is a travesty of the notion of fairness, quite apart from a gross misunderstanding of what constitutes good schooling.

But even more dangerous is the peculiarly lethal principle of "fairness" that seems to prevail in the NHS [National Health Service, the healthcare system of the United Kingdom]: if everyone can't have it, no one should. On this basis, procedures and medications that could save or transform individual lives must be barred if they cannot be made available to every patient who might conceivably benefit from them.

Once again, "fair" must mean "the same": so the breast cancer patient who is a young mother may be denied the drug that could lengthen her life because it would not be feasible to provide it for all the breast cancer patients who are over 80, and if she offers to pay for the drug herself she may be barred from receiving any NHS treatment (because it is "unfair" for her to use her own money to buy what others cannot afford).

How have we come to accept such vindictive uses of the word "fair"?

Of course it was initially the fault of the Left and its special pleading lobbies, which—like some Fairtrade promoters—had a lot to gain. But the Right has been complicit: it has surrendered words like "fairness" and "opportunity"—and accepted caricatures of other words such as "selfish" and "greedy"—with scarcely a murmur of dissent.

Freer Trade Is the Way to Make Trade Fairer

Herbert Oberhaensli

Herbert Oberhaensli is head of economics and international re-lations at Nestlé. This is adapted from "Free and Fair: Making the Progressive Case for Removing Trade Barriers," an essay collection published by the London-based Foreign Policy Centre, a think tank.

The debate about globalization has become increasingly polarized. The anti-globalization or anti-capitalism lobby likes to conjure up images of ruthless corporations urging governments to lower trade barriers in their pursuit for new markets and ever new ways to make a profit. Businesses, particularly those from the industrialized world, they imply, are the only ones to prosper from free trade and so the only ones eager to bring it about. Consumers and workers, meanwhile, pick up the tab. The reality is very different.

There are many beneficiaries and there are many drivers of globalization. In fact, free trade is one of the most powerful guarantors of fair trade, which should be high on the list of anyone really interested in helping the so-called developing countries. To make the world fairer, we need to make trade freer.

The Need to Reduce Trade Barriers

At the moment, we are still living with a trading system that has many forms of open and hidden protectionism, including undue tariff barriers, cumbersome customs procedures and trade distorting subsidies of all kinds. This creates a trading environment that is both far from free and also far from being fair.

Herbert Oberhaensli, "No Fair Trade Without Free Trade," *Wall Street Journal*, November 29, 2004. Reprinted with permission of The Wall Street Journal, conveyed through Copyright Clearance Center, Inc.

Trade-distorting subsidies don't even always work for those they are supposed to protect. The European Union's [EU] Common Agricultural Policy [CAP, a system of European Union farm subsidies and programs] and farm policies of other OECD [Organisation for Economic Co-operation and Development, a group of 30 countries committed to democracy and a market economy] countries are very good examples of this problem. Approximately 70% of EU subsidies go to 30% of the biggest farmers. Most small farmers usually struggle to break even—despite the subsidies.

[Agricultural] protectionism hurts the livelihood of a large part of the more than 3 billion people living in rural areas of the developing world.

Real CAP reform would send a powerful message of free and fair trade to the world as it would end the effective locking out of farmers from developing countries. Latin America and many Asian sugar producers, for instance, who at the moment find it impossible to successfully enter European markets despite being very competitive, could finally sell their goods on the continent. Such free and fair trade would be mutually beneficial: European consumers would be able to buy cheaper products while Latin American and Asian farmers could make a better living. Unfortunately, Europe is not alone in wasting billions in farm subsidies—the U.S. is also guilty of handing out distorting farm aid. America's 25,000 cotton farmers alone receive each year $3.5 billion in subsidies, effectively locking out some of the poorest African countries that could offer American consumers much cheaper cotton of comparable quality. This kind of protectionism hurts the livelihood of a large part of the more than 3 billion people living in rural areas of the developing world.

A constructive free trade agenda would help lift emerging economies out of poverty. This should also include the liberalization of trade between developing countries. Just as free trade helped Switzerland—the home of Nestlé—in the 19th century, free trade can help the developing world in the 21st century. Reducing trade barriers is vital to increase the efficiency of global economic structures and systems and to promote the economic development of some of the world's poorest countries.

Free and Fair Trade Benefits Everyone

In October 2002, Rubens Ricupero, Secretary General of the United Nations Conference on Trade and Development, went so far as to tell international business leaders that their most important corporate social responsibility was to advocate free trade and capacity-building in developing countries. Only when governments lower barriers can local and international companies invest in new capacities, thus attracting investment and improving living standards.

It is certainly right that businesses can gain from globalization but so can emerging economies. The two are not mutually exclusive. The dichotomy of the anti-globalization movement is a false one. But while it is true that lowering trade barriers creates new opportunities, it also intensifies competition. And some businesses are simply afraid of this competition and don't want to adapt to the new challenges, rejecting therefore free trade. The same debate is raging among governments around the world, but as long as they hold on to protectionism they will continue to frustrate economic progress of developing countries.

Contrary to the anti-globalization slogans, there is no single business voice at trade summits and no powerful monolithic force driving the opening of international markets. However, the unambiguous message at the heart of all campaigns for free and fair trade is that it will increase prosperity in both the developing and developed world. This holds the key to the eventual success of future trade talks.

Businesses cannot allow themselves to become bystanders in trade negotiations. They need to develop a strategic, long-term perspective on trade liberalization, appreciating its overall benefits as well as its risks. Strong, balanced and successful advocacy from companies in all sectors and of all sizes, from rich and poor countries, need to muster a common effort to guarantee the proper functioning of the multi-lateral trading system that will emerge from future trade rounds. Before business leaders are able to convince others, however, they may need first of all to convince themselves.

Fair Trade Is Impossible Under Capitalism

Shamus Cooke

Shamus Cooke is a trade union activist. He serves on the editorial board for Workers Compass, an organization that advocates for socialism in the United States.

The global debate around free trade and its consequences have evolved tremendously in recent years, from tiny circles of leftist critics into a mass international protest movement. Although the movement began to bloom in response to polices of the World Trade Organization (WTO [an international agency created by the United Nations to help developing countries by providing loans]), the biggest demonstrations have been in response to the now-popular "bi-lateral" free-trade agreements that economically powerful countries sign with poorer nations. Once one has become conscious of the problems created by free-trade agreements, whether they are international or regional, an immediate [challenge] presents itself: finding a feasible alternative.

Making Trade Fair

Yes, the trade policy advocated by most corporate-submissive politicians is "free trade," and, yes, this policy has had devastating consequences for people in multiple countries, while filling the already-full bank accounts of the rich. But the issue of "free trade" alone isn't sufficient to fully explain the vast social problems so apparent in so many countries.

For example, many progressive-minded people make the seemingly common-sense conclusion that, if free trade is bad, then its opposite, protectionism, must be good. This is not the

Shamus Cooke, "Alternatives to Free Trade: Fair Trade and Beyond," *Socialist Appeal*, June 21 2007. Reproduced by permission.

case. The search, therefore, for a real alternative has led some to attach themselves to the notion of "fair trade." This term means different things to different people, as there is no strict definition on what fair trade is, or what it would look like if actually implemented. The ambiguous definition has attracted a wide range of [adherents], from the honest progressive to the dishonest reactionary. There are progressive sections of the fair trade movement that clearly knows what it doesn't want, but lacks specifics on what it does want, as shown by the Alliance for Responsible Trade:

> "This enormous, unified movement is one of people telling those political leaders, financial speculators and the transnational corporations who promote neoliberal policies that their agenda is unacceptable. It is a movement of people demanding their very humanity. They do so by stating that nutritious food, a comfortable place to live, a clean and healthy environment, health care and education are human rights."

There is extremely progressive content in this quote that should be actively encouraged. But there is something lacking as well. For instance, one might ask, "What exactly is trade, and how do we make it fair?" Ultimately, one cannot "trade" what one does not own. What trade under capitalism really means is that corporations buy commodities owned by other corporations on an international level, eventually to be sold to consumers locally. At bottom, what is unfair is that individuals or small groups of individuals can own corporations—the entities that produce society's vast wealth, not for socially useful proposes, but for profit. Understanding trade must begin here, at the foundation, so that solutions are proposed that don't merely address the effects of the world economic structure, but its cause. A brief outline of the history of the fair trade movement, along with its various challenges and limitations, will help us gain a better perspective on possible solutions to a problem that goes far beyond trade.

The Origins of Fair Trade

The humble origins of the fair trade movement had little to do with politics. The NGOs [nongovernmental organizations] and religious organizations that founded the movement in the 1940s viewed the issue from a humanitarian, philanthropic perspective: third world countries were horribly poor and something needed to be done to help them. The solution the fair-traders devised came from a stark economic fact—people in poor countries seemed to be getting unfairly compensated for the goods they were producing. A hypothetical example is a blanket that took 10 hours to weave, but fetched only three dollars on the world market. To combat this inequity, the fair trade organizations created shops where one could specifically buy handicrafts, and culturally unique goods at "fair" prices. The above-market price offered was considered a donation of sorts, and there remain segments of the fair-trade movement that retain this perspective and limit their focus accordingly.

Of course someone should not get paid three dollars for 10 hours of work. The example of the blanket weaver can be used, on a small level, to explain a crucial economic law that keeps both blanket weavers and poor nations impoverished.

A blanket may cost three dollars to purchase on the international market because machinery was used to eliminate the labor time that makes it more expensive otherwise. So, if a corporation is the first to invent a new machine that saves additional labor time, and the blanket can then be sold for two dollars, a new standard is created internationally. But an interesting thing happens when two corporations with unequal machinery compete on the world market: the inferior corporation spends much more man power, i.e. wealth, than the other—wealth is thus transferred to the countries where there exists highly developed machinery; the countries that have the machinery make handsome profits for their blankets while countries with none receive little or nothing.

There can be no fair trade where vast inequalities in productivity exist, especially when the rich nations have such an immense productivity advantage in machinery, due to the tremendous wealth they've accumulated in past generations through colonialism, slavery, and more recent imperialist military interventions. The advanced machinery that is one example of this accumulated wealth serves only to further distance the rich and poor countries through competition on the world market.

Once a powerful nation has a productive advantage over the majority of other nations, it becomes a champion of free trade, so that its cheaper products may dominate the international market, invading the lesser developed countries and destroying their domestic industries. It was these "deeper causes" [of] inequality that the founding fair-traders were oblivious to, leading eventually to a need for new ideas.

The Attempt to Reform the Market

The "2nd wave" of the fair-trade movement began with a deeper political analysis than its predecessor. An understanding of the international system of trade was developed, including the institutions that helped maintain the unequal status quo. In fact, an overemphasis was developed toward these organizations, ignoring the [already described] economic factors that inevitably make fair trade impossible under capitalism.

The movement's focal point was Europe, where a variety of progressive organizations worked in conjunction with a coalition of third world nations known as "The Group of 77" in an effort to reform the institutions that governed the capitalist system. The height of success in this movement was its formal recognition by the United Nations [UN], which adopted the slogan of "Trade not Aid" at the United Nations Conference on Trade and Development. It amounted to naught. The rich countries that control the UN eventually derailed the movement, through a policy of pitting the poor countries against each other through bribes, concessions, and threats.

This defeat lead to demoralization of the rank and file activists, who, burned by their attempt to reform a major institution of capitalism, chose to refocus their efforts on the more practical grassroots work of "market access." This less-grandiose strategy soon encountered resistance. Not only do large corporations own most of society's wealth but also the means to transport it. Communities of people in the poorer countries who sought to continue their way of life found it increasingly difficult to market the already-decreasing value of their goods. This was typically limited to agricultural goods only, since the small-scale manufacturers had already been destroyed by the invisible hand of the market.

The corporations of the rich countries, constantly bothered by their native workers' demands for higher wages, fled to the third world for relief.

The large corporations that dominated agricultural production did not want competition from smaller outfits and used their connections to the corporations that owned the ports and railways—often it was one [and] the same—to effectively exclude the unconnected. The fair-trade movement focused on the grassroots buying and selling of goods produced by noncorporate groups, villages, or collectives, who were striving to stay alive in a world dominated by large corporations. Many segments of the fair-trade movement continue to align themselves with this approach, and have achieved more than anyone could have expected of them.

Embracing Ethical Consumerism and Labor Unions

As of December 2006, 569 producer organizations in 58 developing countries were fair trade certified. The fair trade label has now found its ways into the supermarkets owned by the super-corporations. The demand for these products—once again, usually at above-market prices—has been enthusiastically received by those able to afford them. A whole political philosophy has evolved from the buying of "socially just" products, known as "consumer activism." The preachers of this philosophy are of course mainly from the middle class, and have been largely unable to expand their beliefs beyond select clothing and agricultural goods. Once again, [people] who considered the concept of fair trade to be worthwhile searched for new ideas that could elevate themselves above the obvious limitations posed by consumer activism.

The current period in the fair-trade movement has grown to encompass new layers of people with a consistently widening perspective; most notably the involvement of labor unions. This came as a result of "globalization," an accelerated process of global, economic integration that capitalism required to maintain its existence. The most crucial aspect of globalization involved the working class of the world: world capitalism had created a situation where the majority of the earth's population lived on actual slave wages; the corporations of the rich countries, constantly bothered by their native workers' demands for higher wages, fled to the third world for relief.

"Fair trade" to the bureaucrats who control the unions is merely protectionism dressed up in radical clothing.

This "corporate flight" in search of slave wages has in turn lowered the wages of workers everywhere. A corporation in the US paying unionized workers cannot compete with one in China paying a dollar a day. Jobs and facilities were shipped overseas, union membership sunk to new lows; the once mighty political power of the unions dissipated. This is how organized labor in the developing countries was drawn into the fair trade movement: out of necessity.

Fair Trade as Protectionism

But "fair trade" to the bureaucrats who control the unions is merely protectionism dressed up in radical clothing; it is the extremely limited, nationalistic solution they offer to the outsourcing of jobs and facilities. Once again, protectionism seems like a common-sense solution: if a company produces a commodity that cannot compete with a foreign company, and the workers wish to keep their jobs, the company's "competitiveness" seems like a priority. And if your political perspective is strictly bound to the tight confines of capitalism, there really is nowhere else to go. It is this slavish submission to the market economy that is proving to be debilitating to workers [and] demanding a wider, internationalist solution.

This "company first, workers second" attitude has led to worker-management "partnerships" that continue to be used to destroy the wages and benefits of workers, setting the union movement back decades. The intent of the partnership philosophy aims at fooling workers into thinking that the enemy is not at home, in the plush homes of the stockholders, but abroad—the companies and workers of foreign countries.

This nationalist ideology not only divides workers but disempowers them, and instead links their fate to governmental policy. If a union's strategy is to beg Congressmen to erect tariff barriers to protect them from cheap Chinese goods, dangerous waters are being entered. The mega-corporations that own these politicians end up asking for the same thing; they view China's rise as a threat to their "strategic interests," i.e., profits. And as history teaches, economic threats are often solved by military means.

This is the ultimate problem with protectionism: it leads to war. This relationship is not direct, but [neither] is it abstract. The link between a nation and the corporations that function within it is unbreakable, as a nation's politics flows from its economy. A government can be instantly destabilized if its economy goes to pieces, and this can happen quickly if the giant corporations that largely constitute a country's economy are suddenly denied—because of protectionist policy—access to another country's market. This is only the most glaring example of how protectionism can cause major economic and political disruptions on an international scale.

In the dog-eat-dog world of profit making and competition, fairness plays absolutely no role.

Already many countries are developing protectionist tendencies similar to those that erupted before WWI and WWII. After WWII, capitalism experienced a prolonged boom, leading to free-trade cooperation in the WTO. Now, the boom is over, and an "everyone for themselves" protectionist mentality has taken over. The abandonment of the WTO is itself an expression of this: the rich countries are done cooperating in the WTO, they are instead opting for regional trade agreements where they can secure the resources and trade leverage desired with poorer countries. These now-popular trading blocs are dominated by specific imperialist powers, such as the European Union (Germany), NAFTA [North Atlantic Free Trade Agreement] (US), CAFTA [Central America Free Trade Agreement] (US), PAFTA [Pan-Arab Free Trade Agreement] (Australia), ASEAN [Association of Southeast Asian Nations] (Japan), and UNASUR [Union of South American Nations] (Brazil). History teaches that trade blocs inevitably turn into military blocs, and war [follows] soon thereafter.

These very real dangers present an urgent question of clarity to those who align themselves with the notion of fair trade. As it stands now, the ideas of fair trade are obscure enough that protectionism is a valid interpretation. This very dangerous perspective must be combated at every opportunity.

Socialism Is the Starting Point

Indeed, throughout its history, fair trade has failed to define the clear political principles needed for developing a strategy capable of achieving its lofty goals. Generally speaking, fair trade has sought to transform capitalism into something it cannot be, demanding a new perspective that can break through the [already described] inevitable restrictions one encounters while trying to reform the market economy. Capitalism cannot be reformed. In the dog-eat-dog world of profit making and competition, fairness plays absolutely no role. Nor can it. If workers' rights, the environment, health care, or human rights restrict profit making, they will be paid lip-service to but ignored nonetheless

The wealth-producing functions of the giant corporations can be transformed into socially useful enterprises, run on a democratic basis, rather than the economic/political totalitarianism produced under private ownership. Running society should be a social task, where everybody has a say into what is produced and how. The political philosophy that best reflects this idea is commonly referred to as socialism, and is the starting point for anyone who wishes to create a truly fair society.

CHAPTER 4

How Can the Fair Trade System Be Improved?

Chapter Preface

Despite the global economic slowdown, the fair trade market continued to grow in 2009. Starbucks Coffee, for example, announced plans to double its fair-trade coffee purchases to 40 million tons in 2009, while Wal-Mart planned to quadruple its purchases of fair trade bananas. The future is expected to bring even more growth. Economic experts have forecasted double-digit growth in fair trade purchases over the next five years in countries including the United States, France, Germany, Italy, the Netherlands, Spain, Sweden, the United Kingdom, Japan, and Australia. Experts say that consumers increasingly want to shop for products grown or made according to ethical standards. The biggest category of ethical consumer products is organic food, but fair trade products are quickly gaining ground as consumer support swells for fair trade principles such as fair prices, fair labor conditions, community development, and environmental sustainability.

Commentators say that much of the recent growth in the fair trade market is the result of the founding of the Fairtrade Labelling Organizations International (FLO) in 1997 and the creation of a uniform fair trade certification and monitoring system that allowed consumers to trust that fair trade guidelines were being followed. As consumer demand for fair trade grows, fair trade certifications are expected to expand to include an increasing number and variety of products. TransFair USA, the U.S. fair trade labeling organization, has indicated that it will certify up to a dozen new products in 2009, including avocados and olive oil, as well as its first non-food commodity—cotton clothing.

The fair trade certification program, however, has encountered some obstacles that may affect the future of fair trade. One issue is that some producers have begun to forgo costly FLO certification while still trading within the fair trade system. Similarly, some larger retailers have opted to create their own fair trade certification programs rather than participate in the FLO system. Fair trade supporters fear that both of these trends may undermine FLO and confuse consumers, many of whom will not know which fair trade label to trust. In addition, as large corporations have begun selling fair-trade-certified products, and often buying from large producers instead of small farmers, many critics suggest that the FLO label is being diluted. Critics argue that the fair trade label is being abused by sellers that do only a little fair trade business in order to improve their public image. Mainstream retailer Starbucks, for example, sells mostly non-fair-trade products but has gotten a significant amount of positive press about its decision to sell some fair trade certified coffee. Whether consumers will continue to trust the fair trade label or begin to view it with skepticism could either help or hinder future growth prospects for the industry.

Even assuming continuing robust growth in the fair trade market, however, this and other types of ethical consumerism are expected by most economists to remain only a small part of overall consumer spending. According to one market expert, for example, ethical consumerism now accounts for only about 3–5 percent of the global market, and at most, may grow to around 7–10 percent over the next several years. Although many fair trade advocates hope that the ethical consumer movement will eventually overtake and change the mainstream market, other commentators suggest that it will never be more than a way for a small segment of wealthy consumers to feel less guilty about their high-consumption lifestyles. In fact, many observers argue that what is needed not an expansion of ethical consumerism, which will always remain a niche market, but rather governmental intervention and policies that will remove unethical choices from the overall market—that is, changes in national and global trade standards. If all agricultural products, for example, were required to be produced according to uniform ethical standards, the playing field would be leveled for all producers. At the same time, consumers would not need to worry about choosing fair trade labels or similar labels or determining which labels can be trusted.

This idea of removing unethical choices from consumers may sound far-fetched given the fact that global trading is today based on the idea of "free trade," which has been concerned with promoting competitive prices and eliminating restrictions on trade. However, a few companies have already begun to use ethical choices as a marketing strategy. One is a huge British department retailer—Marks & Spencer—which launched a social responsibility program in 2007 aimed at dramatically increasing the number of its products produced in sustainable ways. And in the United States, frustrations with free trade have led labor unions and worker advocates to press policy-makers to include fair trade provisions—basically labor and environmental protections—in existing and future free trade agreements between the United States and other countries. Critics of this approach, however, say such protectionist measures would only lead us backward, and that trade must be made even freer in order to become fairer to everyone around the world.

How fair trade should grow and whether fair trade concepts could or should influence the wider consumer market are the focus of the viewpoints in this chapter.

Agricultural Trade Must Be Transformed to Help Small Farmers and Boost Fair Trade

Pacific Ecologist

Pacific Ecologist is part of the family of Ecologist journals and is published by the Pacific Institute of Resource Management (PIRM), an organization founded in 1984 and dedicated to the sustainable use of the earth's resources.

No civilised community should tolerate the extremes of prosperity and poverty caused by trade practices, which deprive and impoverish millions of the world's poorest, report Oxfam and Third World Network Africa. Rich-country members of the WTO, while protecting and subsidising their own domestic producers, force developing countries to open their markets, then dump their heavily subsidised products on them, destroying local food production and food security. Now the European Commission is threatening 76 of the world's poorest countries, trying to force them into trade agreements which could be even more devastating. Reform of world trade is essential to end deep social injustice.

Ninety-six percent of the world's farmers live in developing countries, where agriculture provides the main source of income for 2.5 billion people. Despite growing urbanisation, two-thirds of the world's poor still live in rural areas and nearly three-quarters of the workforce of the Least Developed Countries (LDCS) are employed in agriculture. While demand for food continues to grow in developing countries, 17% of their populations are already under-nourished.

Agriculture in developing countries is critical to food security, poverty reduction, and economic growth. It's therefore crucial agricultural trade rules are designed to foster agriculture in these countries. As developing countries represent two-thirds of the World Trade Organisation's membership, most of the under-nourished people in the world and 96% of its farmers, their proposals, rather than the commercial interests of rich, developed countries and multinational corporations, should be the linchpin of any agreement. Yet, the system which governs world agricultural trade, the Uruguay Round Agreement on Agriculture (AoA), is inherently unjust. It legalises unfair trading practices by rich countries, thereby denying poorer countries the chance to benefit from their share of wealth generated by global trade.

Transnational food companies have a keen interest in ensuring world trade rules place no obstacle on their expansion. It was the former Cargill Vice-president, Dan Amstutz, who drafted the original text of the current agreement on agriculture. Major companies, like Cargill, are particularly keen on opening Southern markets, irrespective of the effects on rural livelihoods and food security:

> Over half the population growth by 2008 will happen in Asia as well as 30% of world income growth in the next decade . . . people in India and Vietnam spend more than half their income on food, while the Chinese spend more than a third. If better food could be delivered more efficiently, more income would be freed up to spend on other things like motorbikes, cell phones, even computers . . . a global open food system would be best where the regions that grow food best are linked through with regions that need food most . . . this describes a region where the best areas for growing food, the Americas, are linked through trade with areas where food is needed most, Asia. (Cargill)

Developing Markets Forced Open

Spectacular double standards are at play in agricultural world trade. Rich-country members of the WTO, while protecting and subsidising their own domestic producers, at the same time force developing countries to open their markets. Haiti, for example, is now one of the most open economies in the world. Under pressure from the IMF [International Monetary Fund, an organization that oversees the global financial system] and the USA, in 1995 it cut its rice tariff from 35% to just 3%. Each year the USA spends $1.3 billion in subsidies to support a rice crop that costs $1.8 billion to grow, making possible the dumping of 4.7 million tonnes of rice on world markets at 34% below production cost, damaging poor countries like Haiti, Ghana and Honduras. Developing countries should be allowed to use policies that allow them to develop fragile farming sectors.

Profits for Riceland Foods of Arkansas, USA, the world's biggest rice mill, rose by $123 million from 2002 to 2003 thanks largely to a 50% increase in exports, much to Haiti, under pressure from the IMF. As a result, rice imports increased by 150% in nine years and today three out of every four plates of rice eaten in Haiti come from the US. Local farmers' livelihoods have been devastated and rice-growing areas now have among the highest levels of malnutrition and poverty. The price of rice in Haiti has hardly fallen, and malnutrition now affects 62% of the population, up from 48% in the early 1980s.

Agricultural trade's main flaw is it has allowed rich countries to dump their subsidy-driven surpluses on world markets, depressing prices so local producers can no longer compete. Developing-country domestic markets are thus undermined, their import dependence increased, and export opportunities denied. US subsidies on cotton, for example, have stimulated overproduction, leading to a slump in cotton prices on the world market. As a consequence, cotton exporting countries in sub-Saharan Africa lost an estimated $301 million in export earnings in the 2001/02 season alone. Millions of African cotton farmers now see their livelihoods under threat.

At the same time, high tariffs in rich countries continue to limit marketing and diversification opportunities for developing countries. As a result, the liberalisation of agricultural markets has mainly benefited the few transnational companies that dominate agricultural trade, and a tiny minority of wealthy landowners in developed countries. Farmers in developing countries captured only 35% of world agricultural exports in 2001, down from 40% in 1961, as a result of falling commodity prices and high trade barriers. The human costs of unfair trade are immense. If Africa, East Asia, South Asia, and Latin America were each to increase their share of world exports by 1%, the resulting income gains could lift 128 million people out of poverty. In Africa alone, this would generate $70 billion, approximately five times the amount Africa receives in aid.

The existing trade system is indefensible and unsustainable.

Undermining Livelihoods in Poor Countries

In their rhetoric, governments of rich countries constantly stress their commitment to poverty reduction. Yet in practice rigged rules and double standards lock poor people out of the benefits of trade, closing the door to an escape route from poverty. For example: rich countries spend $1 billion daily on agricultural subsidies. The resulting surpluses are dumped on world markets, undermining the livelihoods of millions of smallholder farmers in poor countries. When developing countries export to rich-country markets, they face tariff barriers four times higher than those encountered by rich countries. Northern governments reserve their most restrictive trade barriers for the world's poorest people. Trade restrictions in rich countries cost developing countries $100 billion yearly—twice as much as they receive in aid.

- While rich countries keep their markets closed, poor countries have been pressurised by the IMF and the World Bank to open their markets at breakneck speed, often with damaging consequences for poor communities.

- The international community has failed to address the problem of low and unstable commodity prices, which consign millions of people to poverty. Coffee prices, for example, have fallen by 70% since 1997, costing exporters in developing countries $8 billion in lost foreign-exchange earnings.

- Powerful transnational companies (TNCs) are left free to engage in investment and employment practices which increase poverty and insecurity, constrained only by weak voluntary guidelines. In many countries, export-led success is built by exploiting women and girls.

- Many rules of the WTO on intellectual property, investment, and services protect rich countries' interests and powerful TNCs, while imposing huge costs on developing countries. This bias raises fundamental questions about the legitimacy of the WTO.

The existing trade system is indefensible and unsustainable. No civilised community should be willing to tolerate the extremes of prosperity and poverty generated by current trade practices. Large parts of the developing world are becoming enclaves of despair, increasingly marginalised and cut off from the rising wealth generated through trade. Shared prosperity cannot be built on such foundations. Like the economic forces that drive globalisation, the anger and social tensions that accompany vast inequalities in wealth and opportunity will not respect national borders. The instability they generate threatens us all. In today's globalised world, our lives are more inextricably linked than ever before, and so is our prosperity. As a global community, we sink or swim together.

US-European Union Sugar Subsidies Illegal

The US and EU [European Union] are blocking a deal to make trade fair in the Doha Round, in the wake of findings by the WTO that US and EU sugar subsidies are illegal. Oxfam research shows the trade superpowers are illegally subsidising a slew of products, amounting to $13 billion, from butter to orange juice, to tobacco butter to orange juice, to tobacco and tomatoes, from corn to rice. There are other subsidies worth billions more.

Reform of world trade is only one requirement for ending the deep social injustices that pervade globalisation. Action is also needed to reduce inequalities in health, education, and the distribution of income and opportunity, including inequalities that exist between women and men. However, world trade rules are a key part of the poverty problem; fundamental reforms are needed to make them part of the solution. For example, corn producers around the world would gain as much in higher prices from the abolition of the US illegal corn subsidies as the UN estimates is needed yearly for health projects that would prevent the death of 3 million infants annually.

Instead of doing the right thing and removing subsidies, rich countries are trying to use regional and bilateral trade deals to attain concessions they cannot get at the WTO, with serious implications for poor countries' development, says a new report published by Oxfam in March 2007. Twenty-five developing countries have now signed free trade deals with developed countries, with more under negotiation, according to the report, Signing Away the Future. There are more than 250 regional or bilateral trade agreements in force, governing 30% of world trade.

"Trade is important but these agreements are bad, requiring enormous irreversible concessions from developing countries and almost nothing in return from rich countries," said Celine Charveriat, head of Oxfam's Make Trade Fair campaign. "These deals demand much faster liberalisation and stricter intellectual property rules than the WTO. They strip developing countries of the right to govern their economies and threaten their abilities to protect their poorest people and lift them out of poverty," she added. The report highlights a number of ways free trade deals can be harmful:

- Investment rules in free trade agreements and bilateral investment treaties deny governments the right to protect workers, the environment and the economy, and can expose them to compensation claims that reach billions.

- Stricter intellectual property provisions threaten to deny poor people access to affordable medicines, undermine traditional farming methods, and remove rights to traditional knowledge.

- Harsh tariff liberalisation threatens farmers' livelihoods and will impede future economic development.

- The web of different agreements undermines multilateralism and diverts trade.

Meanwhile, a study commissioned by the EU has predicted a proposed Economic Partnership Agreement with West Africa will lead to import surges of over 15% on key commodities, like onions, potatoes, beef and poultry, which will devastate the rural sector.

Charveriat: "Poor countries are being pressured to open their markets dramatically through free trade agreements, but developed countries do not even have to touch their massive agricultural subsidies that lead to overproduction and dumping. It's hugely unjust."

An Independent Watchdog Is Needed to Regulate the Global Food Market

Chris Mercer

Chris Mercer is editor on BeverageDaily.com and DairyReporter-.com. He has also produced material for the BBC, Sunday Telegraph, *and other media.*

Growing consumer awareness and concern about sustainable and ethical food sourcing is putting firms in industries like coffee and cocoa under pressure.

Images of striking cocoa farmers in Ivory Coast were last week beamed around the world, while a new film, *Black Gold,* vividly depicts the poverty and uncertainty in the lives of Ethiopian coffee producers.

Coverage like this has seen ethical food sales rise strongly in several developed markets. Shoppers in the UK [United Kingdom] alone were set to spend more than £2bn [2 billion British pounds] on ethical foods this year, up 62 percent from 2002, according to a recent report from [market researcher] *Mintel.* It said spending would double again in five years.

The Fairtrade Label Is Not Enough

The various certification schemes that allow consumers to make this choice are not going to be a viable option for the whole market, however, whether we are talking coffee, cocoa or cut flowers.

Don't get me wrong, I believe a lot of people have done a lot of good work to promote schemes like Fairtrade, which have helped to drag ethical and sustainable issues into the public spotlight.

But now we stand at a crossroads. The Fairtrade label will continue to grow and may develop further into an almost super-ethical niche sector, but it and other schemes like it still [make up only] a minuscule amount of the market.

Most coffee farmers, meanwhile, are still being paid less for their beans than they were 20 years ago, according to International Coffee Organisation figures. The gap between retail and grower prices also remains large.

Establishing a new international watchdog to regulate the global supply chain would provide a framework to make trade fairer, more professional and more organised.

There is a moral argument too, of course. How can anybody claim humans to be a civilised, advanced race in a world where the United Nations says 40 countries face acute food shortages and developing countries have actually [become] poorer?

And, on a more practical note, there is that small question of impending ecological disaster, predicted by several top scientists. Yet, it is absurd to demand that developing countries manage their environment responsibly when they do not even have enough to eat.

It seems clear that we need a broader approach on trade. The food chain has gone global, but regulation and controls have struggled to keep pace.

An International Watchdog Needed

Establishing a new international watchdog to regulate the global supply chain would provide a framework to make trade fairer, more professional and more organised. The United Nations would be an obvious body to play a key role in this, although co-operation from countries, trading blocs and food firms would inevitably be necessary for it to carry any weight.

Yes, food firms and retailers will likely have to make greater commitments to ensure suppliers are treated fairly, and, yes, this may cost money. With power must come responsibility, and public concerns over sustainable and ethical sourcing are not going to die down.

But, industry would be wrong to assume such a watchdog would act against its interest. It could, for example, provide independent tribunals for disputes between companies and producers, going some way to releasing firms from inevitable accusations of underhand tactics.

Current unrest among cocoa workers in Ivory Coast may have been quelled sooner using this approach.

It would also provide a wider certification system for companies to display their ethical credentials, escaping the complaint among some in the industry that the Fairtrade scheme effectively labels everyone outside it as unfair traders.

Extra schemes providing benefits to producers and suppliers would be free to exist, but this is about establishing a baseline in the sector.

For consumers, an independent supply chain regulator would improve transparency in the chain, enabling them to more easily make an ethical shopping choice.

For producers, an independent regulator could provide a framework for meaningful change on a broader scale. It would make the supply chain more professional by introducing minimum, uniform standards and rules.

And, a development working group including top food processing, technology and packaging professionals, could help producers to examine ways to improve their lot. With commodities and cocoa, this may be to help producers bag more profit by processing beans in their own country instead of handing them straight over.

Other initiatives should and must work alongside greater international regulation. For example, Europe's coffee industry is expecting to launch the 4C scheme, which will establish a Common Code for the Coffee Community.

This is a potentially ground-breaking move involving most of the big coffee firms in Europe, and it deserves a mention here, although producers in some countries have privately expressed skepticism.

Greater international regulation could help schemes like this to flourish. In a world that has become increasingly obsessive over the advantages of a free market system, we often forget that several thinkers intended regulation to be a key part of this economic model.

A New Label Could Better Help People in Developing Countries

Evelyn Spence

Evelyn Spence is a contributor to Delicious Living *and an editor at* Backpacker *magazine.*

Rajah Banerjee, the owner of the Makaibari tea garden in India's rural Darjeeling hills, started a computer center for local children. La Cooperativa de Trabajadores del Sur, a banana cooperative in southern Costa Rica, installed recycling systems and purchased long-awaited school supplies for the area's kids. The 35,000-member Kuapa Kokoo cooperative in Ghana, which grows and sells cocoa, bought new scales, gained access to banking and credit services, and now has true pride in its Twi-language motto: Pa Pa Paa ("the best of the best"). There are similar stories coming out of Ethiopia, Colombia, East Timor, Brazil, and Thailand. But what unifies them isn't an influx of developed-world aid or an odd lucky strike. These farmers all grow and sell fair-trade-certified goods, and, as a result, they are able to live lives that most of us take for granted—with safe working conditions, honest compensation, and, above all, dignity.

Seeds of Fairness

As an idea, fair trade—with principles like guaranteed minimum prices, sustainable farming methods, prohibition of forced and inappropriate child labor, and direct trade—has been around since 1946, when the Mennonites, through a nonprofit now called Ten Thousand Villages, created a supply chain for handicrafts made in the developing world. The first so-called Worldshop, run by volunteers protesting European colonialism and hoping to lift up underdeveloped regions, opened in the Netherlands in 1969.

But these outposts were inconvenient for consumers and too specialized to gain momentum, and it wasn't until 1988 that a solution was found: What about creating a label to mark everything that is truly fair-trade-produced and then distributing those products worldwide? The first initiative brought coffee from Mexico to mainstream stores in the Netherlands.

Since then, the idea has picked up hundreds of thousands of devotees. In 1998, when TransFair USA unveiled its certification label, it imported 76,000 pounds of coffee from growers in Central and South America and Africa. By 2006, "Fair Trade Certified" was stamped on 64.7 million pounds of beans, representing 7 percent of gourmet coffee's market share. Cocoa, which was certified in 2002, has jumped from 14,000 pounds to 1.8 million pounds in five years. And fair-trade tea increased 187 percent in 2005 and continues to thrive.

Gaining Ground

In the United States, you can now buy fair-trade vanilla, rice, sugar, bananas, mangoes, pineapples, and even soccer balls. In Europe, the list of stuff tagged with the International Fairtrade Certification mark is even more extensive: honey, herbs and spices, fruit juice, nuts, flowers, quinoa, and wine, to name a few.

Since you can't fly to Rwanda or Nicaragua to sample coffee, fair trade provides that link.

In some ways, Europe's jumpstart is merely a reflection of broader differences in cultures and politics. "In general, Europeans are more globally aware," says Reem Rahim, co-founder of Numi Tea, a fair-trade purchaser. "They have more of a pulse on other countries, politically and socially—whereas here, people are generally more isolated, and a smaller percentage are global citizens."

Rodney North, spokesman for Equal Exchange, the oldest U.S. fair-trade coffee company, thinks that Europe's colonial past has influenced Europeans' awareness of being tied economically to the fates of millions of farmers in former colonies. "They're less enamored with free-market capitalism and quicker to see when the free market pits the poor in a losing battle with rich and powerful corporations," he says.

But fair trade is picking up serious momentum in the United States, too—in part on the heels of the booming organic industry, which totaled $15.7 billion in sales in 2006, according to *Nutrition Business Journal*. "More and more people want to know, 'Where does my food come from?'" says Anthony Marek of TransFair USA. He points to the huge increase in U.S. farmers' markets, which have doubled in number since 1994. "You can get back to the basics and look people in the eye. And since you can't fly to Rwanda or Nicaragua to sample coffee, fair trade provides that link."

In a few years, proponents hope that fair-trade designation will be more clearly defined.

What's to Come

There are still some growing pains to deal with, however—mostly in unifying the standards of what makes fair trade fair. Though TransFair USA's Fair Trade Certified label is the most ubiquitous, it's not yet a true national, consensus-based certification program—it certifies a limited number of products and works with a specific list of farms and growers. In response, third-party certifier SCS Certified, Numi, and a few other organizations unveiled a new label in March 2007, with the tagline "Fair Labor Practices and Community Benefits."

"Some of our longtime qualified gardens were left off TransFair's lists and couldn't get their seal, and it didn't seem fair," says Rahim. "We need the system to open more doors."

Whole Foods recently launched Whole Trade—which recognizes companies that adhere to fair labor practices—with the goal of having 50 percent of its imported products qualify. Another initiative, called Domestic Fair Trade, aims to translate international fair-trade principles into local arenas, so small farmers in the United States can be treated the same way as, say, sugar cooperative members in Malawi. And while they aren't officially certified yet, there are already some products (roasted pecans, dried cranberries, tamari almonds) on the shelves. "Trade should be fair no matter where it takes place," says Erbin Crowell, Equal Exchange's domestic fair-trade manager. "Local attention is the next big step."

If you're confused by the number of players, you're not alone: The United States doesn't yet have a truly national, transparent certification scheme. "Right now, consumers are overwhelmed by labels," says Ted Howes, a VP at SCS Certified. "They're thinking, 'Are all these things the same?'"

In a few years, proponents hope that fair-trade designation will be more clearly defined. And whether they sell wine, flowers, or macadamia nuts, as long as growers are fair and want to get certified for it, they can. "Before we know it, these principles will apply worldwide," says Rahim. That means that a stroll down the grocery aisles will come closer to the ideal of meeting the people, face to face, who produce what we eat and drink.

For now, your best bet is to research any new label you see, decide what issue is most important to you, and try to learn about the people who produce, process, and sell what you buy. "We think there's a positive side to globalization," says Marek. "And that's when it turns into a global farmers' market."

Stronger Trade Agreements Are Needed to Guarantee Labor and Environmental Rights

Stephen Coats

Stephen Coats is the director of the U.S. Labor Education in the Americas Project, an organization that supports Latin American workers who are fighting to overcome poverty and make a better life for their families.

Consumers in the US have grown more concerned about and aware of the conditions under which the goods we purchase are produced. This increased consciousness has led to new models of production and consumption, and a variety of alternative product labels with respect to environmental issues (shade-grown coffee), health (organic produce), animal treatment (free-range chickens), and other concerns. Labels are intended to provide an easy way for consumers to know which products reflect our values.

These trends are now being extended to working conditions and the treatment of workers. In large part as a result of campaigns and news stories about sweatshops in the clothing industry, child labor in the coffee and banana sectors, and slave labor on cocoa plantations, companies have become increasingly concerned about their "brand image." Consequently, a number of programs have emerged that certify that a product is produced under acceptable conditions of work.

Using consumer demand to push for better working conditions has proved to be a powerful approach; the "sweat-free" movement, fueled by college activists and workers' rights advocates working together, has permanently raised the bar on

Stephen Coats, "On Beyond Coffee: Fair Trade and Workers' Rights in a Changing Economy," *Peacework*, April 2009. Reproduced by permission.

what it means to be a "socially responsible" company. Through its Designated Suppliers Program, the anti-sweatshop movement created a set of standards, adopted by a growing number of universities and some municipalities, requiring that the goods purchased by these large institutions be bought from unionized or cooperative producers.

Fair Food

The most prominent consumer-oriented social certification in the US is Fair Trade, with a black and white label showing a figure holding evenly balanced scales. In the US, this label is managed by TransFair USA, a member of a consortium called the Fairtrade Labelling Organizations International which controls the label globally.

Non-profit groups interested in improving the conditions of small coffee farmers originated the Fair Trade movement in Western Europe. It has now expanded to other products and begun to evolve out of its origins as an "alternative" market into the mainstream. Fair Trade is a rapidly growing business, expanding its certification beyond coffee and cocoa to bananas, pineapples, and flowers, with plans to certify apparel.

Fair Trade activists sought out small, independent farms and cooperatives, and provided them with a way to reach consumers more directly, thus increasing their profits. Producers in the Fair Trade network are guaranteed a minimum price for their products, and also receive a cash "premium" to use as they wish—often this allows for improvements to production methods and to community services. In return for paying the higher price all this entails, consumers are guaranteed that the producers of their coffee were paid fairly and not deprived of their right to organize.

However, responding in part to growing consumer demand, Fair Trade has in recent years begun to certify food grown by different kinds of producers. For instance, almost all bananas imported to the US—a recent expansion area for Fair

Trade—are grown on Latin American plantations, not on small farms or cooperatives. Some of the plantations which have earned the Fair Trade certification employ hundreds of workers.

> *While Fair Trade certification is an important instrument for making positive change, the most fundamental issue for workers in the Global South is the rules of global trade.*

While Fair Trade has added new criteria for certification that includes how the workers are treated and respect for their basic rights, the expansion of the Fair Trade model to large-scale producers has raised concerns in the labor movement, particularly with banana unions in Latin America (banana production is the most thoroughly unionized sector in Central America, with many active unions working in effective coalitions across national and ideological boundaries). Long-time Fair Trade supporters have raised additional concerns, including opposition to certification of products marketed by transnational corporations (e.g., Dole bananas or Starbucks coffee) and whether Fair Trade has erred in moving beyond small-scale producers to large employers like the banana plantations. These questions are being debated by trade unionists, representatives of the Fair Trade networks, and global labor activists, in an attempt to find a course that promotes environmental sustainability, human rights, *and* growth for the promising "Fair Trade" sector.

The Global Picture

While Fair Trade certification is an important instrument for making positive change, the most fundamental issue for workers in the Global South is the rules of global trade. The terms of international trade agreements have an enormous impact on the lives and working conditions of the world's producers.

We need strong trade rules protecting workers' right to organize in order for workers in every sector to achieve the kind of conditions that Fair Trade certifies.

Workers are extremely vulnerable to exploitation right now.

In this area, we have lost a lot of important ground with the passage of NAFTA [North American Free Trade Agreement] and CAFTA [Central American Free Trade Agreement], international agreements that represent steps backward in the US's ability to push for the enforcement of international labor standards. For instance, in 1999 when seven Guatemalan union leaders were threatened with murder and fled to the US, the US acted in accordance with existing trade law and withheld Guatemala's trade benefits until the Guatemalan government had apprehended and tried the unionists' attackers. Since the passage of CAFTA, however, there has been a resurgence in anti-labor violence in Guatemala (four trade unionists were assassinated in 2007 and another five in 2008, with no charges brought in any of the cases) and the US has not been able to apply any meaningful trade pressure to hold the Guatemalan government accountable.

As Fair Trade activists have recognized from the beginning, workers' rights and environmental sustainability are inseparable.

For those of us in the US, this is a key moment to focus on the terms of global trade. While this issue is not yet foremost on the new [Barack Obama] administration's agenda, the debate is being framed for the consideration of several "bilateral" agreements between the US and other countries. Four agreements were negotiated by the [George W.] Bush administration. Only one, the Peru Agreement, has been passed.

The good news is that these agreements are stronger than NAFTA and CAFTA on the protection of workers' rights. The bad news is that they still aren't strong enough. The Peru Agreement went into effect on February 1 of 2009, so this is an area for close observation.

Sustainability on the Line

Workers are extremely vulnerable to exploitation right now. In 2005, the international Agreement on Textiles and Clothing (also known as the "Multifibre Agreement") came to an end. For 20 years this pact had provided quotas for the amount of clothing that each developing nation could export to wealthier European and North American markets. The World Trade Organization's decision to phase it out has ushered in a period of intense competition among exporter nations, which translates as a "race to the bottom" to reduce labor costs. To this, of course, has been added the impact of the global recession, causing downward pressure on wages and working conditions for workers.

As Fair Trade activists have recognized from the beginning, workers' rights and environmental sustainability are inseparable. In Latin America, banana workers' unions understand this as well, and have been organizing to make the cultivation of bananas more biologically stable (bananas are grown in a monoculture which makes them particularly vulnerable to disease) and less destructive of ecosystems in the communities where the workers make their homes. To wield our greatest power as consumers, we must not only pay a surcharge on some items to cover their real cost—we must also drop a dime and call our Congress members. We need to hold our governments accountable for strong labor and environmental standards in the agreements that increasingly regulate all global trade, fair and otherwise.

Legally Enforceable Global Labor Standards Are Needed to Truly Support Workers

Colin Roche

Colin Roche is campaigns and advocacy executive with Oxfam Ireland, a humanitarian and development organization.

The buying power of consumers can make a difference for [the] world's poor. A couple of weeks before Christmas, British supermarket retailer Sainsbury's decided to switch all their banana sales to bananas carrying the Fairtrade Mark.

This means that small farmers in the Windward Islands in the Caribbean as well as other producers in Latin America will get a better deal and real improvements in their livelihoods.

But much more needs to be done to give producers everywhere a decent living free from poverty.

A Growing Fairtrade Market

This latest move comes after another year of growth for the Fairtrade movement. Consumers across the world are, in ever increasing numbers, demanding to know whether the products they purchase are being produced ethically and companies are responding.

The Fairtrade Mark—an independently run certification guaranteeing fair conditions for workers and producers in the developing world—is now on goods sold in 20 countries worth over €1bn [one billion euros] in 2005.

Millions of producers in Africa, Asia and Latin America now benefit from Fairtrade purchases.

Here in Ireland, sales of goods carrying the Fairtrade Mark are now increasing at a rate of 30pc [percent] a year.

Nearly one in three people, in a survey carried out for Fairtrade Mark Ireland earlier this year, said they had bought a Fairtrade product within the previous four weeks.

Irish companies are part of this trend. Since the first tonne of coffee bought on Fairtrade terms was imported by Bewley's in 1996, Irish companies have seen the benefit of supplying and selling Fairtrade products.

These include companies such as the coffee chain Insomnia, which last September joined other café groups in serving 100pc of their coffee on Fairtrade terms.

Even the famously cost-conscious [airline] Ryanair is now serving Fairtrade tea and coffee on all its flights. Goods with the Fairtrade Mark can now be found in virtually every supermarket in the country.

Long Hours and Abuses

But it's not enough. There are still millions of workers and producers who continue to work in appalling conditions for little reward—often to supply the companies and supermarkets in our cities and towns.

> *Investigations . . . regularly reveal [labour] abuses across the developing world in industries supplying companies in Europe, North America and elsewhere.*

In the same week as the Sainsbury's announcement to stock Fairtrade bananas, British charity War on Want published a report into factories supplying retailers Asda, Tesco and Primark ([JCPenney] in Ireland).

They found extremely long hours—regularly 80 hours a week, six- and seven-day working weeks and wages of as little as 7c [cents] an hour.

This is depressingly familiar.

Investigations by trade unions and development organisations regularly reveal abuses across the developing world in industries supplying companies in Europe, North America and elsewhere.

Ultimately what is required are adequate, legally enforced labour standards everywhere—so that . . . workers are treated with respect and dignity and paid a decent wage.

Research on the sportswear industry, published by Oxfam [an antipoverty group] last summer, also found widespread labour rights abuses in firms producing household brands.

Much more needs to be done, by consumers, companies and governments.

Changes in Trade Rules Needed

While a change in consumer purchases is one hugely important response (for example, to the challenges of labour rights in factories), ultimately what is required are adequate, legally enforced labour standards everywhere—so that no matter where goods are sourced from, or by whom, workers are treated with respect and dignity and paid a decent wage.

This needs to be matched by a framework for global trade which ties the opportunities provided by global commerce to generate wealth to the responsibility to ensure that it benefits those living in poverty.

The rules governing international trade continue to be written in the interests of the richer countries.

The US is pushing Free Trade Agreements which will favour pharmaceutical companies at the expense of poor countries.

In Peru, for example, the cost of medicines is set to double over ten years if their free trade agreement with the US is passed.

The EU [European Union] is pushing for agreements with a host of African, Caribbean and Pacific states which risk serious damage to jobs, livelihoods and government revenue in some of the poorest countries in the world.

Without rules which are fair, then growth and, importantly, pro-poor growth will be hobbled from the start.

But even without fairer trade rules and enforceable laws, what we do each day matters.

It matters to the men and women, often thousands of miles away who grew, picked, sewed or packed the product unseen, for our consumption.

When we buy what they've grown, we can choose to support standards which respect their rights and the environment and give them a decent living by buying Fairtrade.

For companies, there simply is no excuse for sourcing goods from farms or factories where workers are abused.

Sainsbury's and others before them have set an example which more and more companies need to follow. Here in Ireland, Fairtrade banana sales have been increasing, but remain a very small part of the banana market.

No supermarket has made a commitment to stock 100pc Fairtrade. Sainsbury's has shown that it can be done and it should be done on bananas and on other products.

Much more important than a Christmas present, it shows that we can improve the lives of people the whole year round. For the millions who supplied our festive feasts, they deserve nothing less.

America Must Embrace Fair Trade Agreements to Protect American Workers

Virg Bernero

Virg Bernero is the mayor of Lansing, Michigan, and chairman of the Mayors and Municipalities Automotive Coalition (MMAC).

While America reels from the worst economic crisis since the Great Depression, it is time that we take a deeper look at the root causes of our current predicament.

The cold, hard truth is that the unholy alliance between Washington and Wall Street has sold out the American worker and exported our standard of living.

Driven by the insatiable greed of Wall Street profiteers and accelerated by the false promise of free trade, our manufacturing base has been chased out of this country and along with it the livelihood of millions of hard-working Americans.

The Result of Free Trade

It's fashionable these days among the politicians, pundits and so-called experts to claim that free trade is actually good for us. They say it enables us to buy cheaper goods made with cheap foreign labor and this, in turn, raises our standard of living.

With all due respect, the free traders need to ask themselves a more fundamental question: how will Americans buy those goods when they don't even have a paycheck that covers their mortgage, much less the college tuition for their children?

Virg Bernero, "Commentary: Free Trade Has Sold Out the American Worker," *CNN.com*, February 9, 2009. © 2008 Cable News Network. Reproduced by permission.

More than one pundit has told me I need to take a broader view. As the mayor of one of America's countless manufacturing communities, the only view that matters is the one my citizens see every day: Record job losses, home foreclosures and, thanks to the Wall Street wizards, a credit crunch so severe that it is nearly impossible to finance a new car.

This isn't a predicament faced just by Michigan or the Midwest. This is the story of America, told in thousands of desperate households from Connecticut to California.

The pundits claim our manufacturing sector is a relic of the old economy. We're told that we just can't compete anymore. We're told that our future is in the service economy, that jobs in health care and finance and knowledge-based industries will re-create the prosperity our nation once knew.

The truth is that our industrial heritage is an example of everything that was right with our nation's economy. Good jobs with good benefits created the middle class in this country, and now it is being systematically dismantled under the banner of free trade and globalism.

The Case for Fair Trade

Those who continue to espouse free trade ominously warn that protectionism is the wrong path for our nation; that challenging the holy doctrine of free trade invites a global trade war.

Yet we already face rampant protectionism across the globe. Pursuing a free trade agenda in a protectionist world is tantamount to unilateral disarmament.

Our trading partners routinely employ taxes, tariffs and subsidies that underwrite their exports and restrict American products from entering their home markets. They use currency manipulation to reduce the relative cost of their goods here in the USA.

The fact is we're not competing against other companies; we're competing against other countries. I've toured the Hyundai plant in Asan, [South] Korea. The [South] Koreans are wonderful people, but their technology isn't any better and they're not working any harder than Americans.

The difference is that Hyundai doesn't have to pay legacy costs. The [South] Korean government takes care of their retirees. Hyundai doesn't pay health care costs because they have national heath care. If you don't think that's an unfair advantage, you're kidding yourself.

Many Americans are unaware that China sold 10 million cars last year—more than General Motors or Toyota. I can assure you the Chinese government is part and parcel of that success. They're involved in their industry. The [South] Korean government is involved in their industry.

We need . . . [to provide] jobs and economic security to the millions of hard-working American families who have been sold down the river by unfair trade policies.

If we are going to have any chance to compete globally, our government must get involved in our industry and help us rebuild America's industrial might before it is too late.

There's no question that we need this stimulus package [enormous set of tax cuts and spending passed by U.S. Congress in early 2009]. We need the reinvestment in America's infrastructure and in the working people of this country. We need tax cuts delivered directly to the American worker. We need education and retraining for the "green collar" jobs of the future.

But we need more than a short-term shot in the arm. We need a long-term strategy to rebuild the American economy that provides jobs and economic security to the millions of hard-working American families who have been sold down the river by unfair trade policies.

We need fair trade agreements so that the most productive workers in the world—American workers—can put their skills to work and compete in the global economy.

We recently watched our athletes successfully compete in the Olympics against nations of the world. When the playing field is level, Americans can compete against the best from any nation. With fair trade instead of free trade, American workers can once again bring home the gold.

World Leaders Should Take a Strong Stand Against U.S. Protectionism

Steve Charnovitz

Steve Charnovitz is an associate professor at George Washington University Law School and has written extensively on international trade issues.

The motto of the G20 [referring to nineteen of the world's largest economies plus the European Union] . . . [April 12, 2009] . . . London Summit is "Stability Growth Jobs." The world economy is producing an insufficient amount of all three of these economic virtues and so it is appropriate for powerful governments to get together in London to try to improve and coordinate their social, economic, and environmental policies.

The most important thing the G20 leaders can do is to take a strong stand against trade protectionism. A hundred years of economic history has shown that the erection of import barriers diminishes economic growth and creates instability. While tariff and non-tariff barriers can "save" some jobs from import competition, such policies will necessarily reduce other jobs in companies that depend on imports or exports. Although the net effect of protectionist policies on the quantity of jobs is impossible to predict, we do know that the inefficiencies of protection lower the aggregate real income to workers through labor markets.

Thus, promoting freer trade should be a core component of any international plan to promote long-term global eco-

Steve Charnovitz, "Rebuilding Global Trade: Proposals for a Fairer, More Sustainable Future," Geneva, Switzerland: International Centre for Trade and Sustainable Development and the Global Economic Goverance Programme, 2009. Copyright: ICTSD, GEG and individual contributing authors, 2009. Reproduced by permission of the author and publisher.

nomic prosperity. Trade needs to be accompanied by complementary policies on saving and investment, technology, corporate governance, training, education, health, energy, and public infrastructure. Moreover, governments need to coordinate these various policies domestically and internationally so that they do not work at cross purpose. No policy should be used in the short run, for example, trade restrictions or wasteful government spending, that does not also make sense in the long run.

The [Barack] Obama Administration and the new Congress have been quick to adopt protectionist policies.

U.S. Protectionism

All G20 countries should be the object of the G20 recommendations, but the government most in need of external normative pressure from other governments is the United States. That's so for several reasons: First the United States has the largest and wealthiest economy at the G20 meeting and therefore has the weakest excuse to adopt beggar-thy-neighbor policies. Second, if the United States gives in to sirens [enticements] of protection, other countries as a practical matter will find it much harder to resist. Third, as a result of the 2008 election, the Democratic party in the United States has gained firm control of the Congress and the Executive Branch, and so the usual internal checks and balances against wasteful and counterproductive policies have been attenuated.

Vibrant world trade and a strong World Trade Organization (WTO) [an international body that regulates world trade] are terrible things to waste. And yet the [Barack] Obama Administration and the new Congress have been quick to adopt protectionist policies, some of which violate WTO rules.

"Buy American" Provisions

Consider the American Recovery and Reinvestment Act of 2009, better known as the First Obama Stimulus. As the title indicates, the new law is inward looking. The Act has 20 titles, none of which recognize, at least in name, the rest of the world or the interdependence of the US within the world economy. Perhaps the most notorious provision of the Act is Section 1605 titled "Buy American." According to this provision, with certain exceptions, "None of the funds appropriated or otherwise made available by this Act may be used for a project for the construction, alteration, maintenance, or repair of a public building or public work unless all of the iron, steel, and manufactured goods used in the project are produced in the United States." In those 51 words, the Congress and Obama Administration repudiate the benefits of open trade and embrace domestic content policies that will make it harder for the US economy to stabilize, grow, and create good jobs. Those cruel words also send a signal to private social and economic actors in the United States that discriminating against America's trading partners is now thought by Washington elites to be good governance.

In addition to being bad for the US taxpayer and bad for countries that produce manufactured goods and steel, the Buy American provision, if implemented, also violates WTO rules. While it is true that the Act has a provision saying that it "shall be applied in a manner consistent with United States obligations under international agreements," any application of the provision to make the subsidies conditional on domestic content is a *per se* [intrinsic] violation of the WTO Agreement on Subsidies and Countervailing Measures (SCM), Article 3.1(b). The Act was signed into law on February 17, 2009 by the President who urged that the funds be disseminated quickly. One can only assume that serious WTO violations by the United States are already occurring. . . .

Other U.S. Protectionist Tendencies

In addition to the Economic Stimulus Act, the Obama Administration has signaled that it will continue the policies of the [George W.] Bush Administration in bailing out US manufacturers, such as automobile companies, that request financial aid. Subsidies to domestic firms are not per se WTO violations, but can violate the SCM Agreement if they cause adverse effects on other WTO members by promoting the relative competitiveness of exports or reducing the competitiveness of imports. On March 11, 2009, US Representative Sander Levin, a Michigan Democrat and chair of the House Trade subcommittee, defended such subsidies by saying that "In this time of crisis, countries also need the temporary flexibility to help rescue their own industries—through loans, incentives, and regulations—without charges of 'protectionism.' Yet in the same speech, he also called for "the creation of an interagency team led by the Department of Commerce and USTR [Office of the U.S. Trade Representative] to investigate subsidies by leading trade partners." Presumably other G20 countries are now considering whether to ask their agencies to investigate US subsidies to see if they are actionable or countervailable [can be reversed] under the SCM Agreement.

There are no truly "successful" examples of labor provisions in any of the existing US free trade agreements.

The new 2009 Trade Policy Agenda issued by the Obama Administration on March 2, 2009, sends a mixed message. On the one hand, the President's Trade Agenda states that "The President's approach will be to promote adherence to the rule-based international trading system in order to promote economic stability, while introducing new concepts—including increasing transparency and promoting broader participation in the debate—to help revitalize economic growth and promote higher living standards at home and abroad" (page 1).

Yet this positive message is not backed up with anything concrete such as a commitment by the United States to follow WTO rules and comply with the numerous WTO decisions in which the United States was found to be a scofflaw. These included decisions on cases of anti-dumping, *Cotton, Stainless Steel, and Gambling*. Embarrassingly, the United States has lost more WTO disputes as a defendant than any other G20 country. Nor did the Administration take the opportunity in its 2009 Trade Agenda to publicly pledge its long overdue compliance with Mexico's 2001 case against the United States on trucking services under the North American Free Trade Agreement (NAFTA). Even worse, in early March 2009, the Obama Administration gave the go-ahead to the Congress to cut off funds for the cross-border trucking pilot project that had been launched by the [George W.] Bush Administration to show that Mexican trucks do not present a safety hazard to the United States. The Administration also signed onto legislative provisions serving to maintain nontariff barriers on certain poultry imports from China and beef or lamb from Argentina.

Because trade is so beneficial, the G20 should . . . call on the United States to back away from its recent protectionist tendencies.

Labor and Environment Provisions

The Obama Administration has been timid on the issue of securing Congressional approval of the three pending US free trade agreements with Colombia, Panama, and [South] Korea. To be sure, Senator Obama made clear in his campaign that he did not support these agreements. But many observers had hoped that once he became President he would adopt a more centrist position on trade. Perhaps he will, but so far the President's Trade Agenda pledges only that "We are in the process of developing a plan of action to address the pending trade agreements in consultation with the Congress" and that "we will promptly, but responsibly, address the issues surrounding the Colombia, [South] Korea and Panama Free Trade Agreements."

On labor, the "President's Trade Agenda" states: "To make support for global markets sustainable, our consideration of the effects of trade can not stop at the edge of our borders. Trade is more beneficial for the world, and fairer for everyone, if it respects the basic rights of workers. Our trade policies should build on the successful examples of labor provisions in some of our existing agreements."

As someone who has worked on labor rights and trade for 32 years, let me make a few comments about that puzzling paragraph. First, trade is an economic transaction, not a human being, and so trade itself cannot respect or fail to respect the basic rights of workers. Instead protecting the basic rights of workers is the role of governments, the private sector, and the voluntary nongovernmental sector. Sadly, the United States government has been derelict in failing to ratify the ILO [International Labor Organization] Convention on Freedom of Association and the Right to Organize which has been sitting on a dusty shelf in the US Senate since 1949. On labor policy and on foreign policy, the Obama Administration should be judged on whether it asks the Senate to approve this treaty, which has been ratified by Colombia and Panama (but not South Korea). Second, there are no truly "successful" examples of labor provisions in any of the existing US free trade agreements. Of course, every US free trade agreement (except [with] Israel) contains a labor chapter or side agreement. But the only labor language within a free trade agreement that has produced anything at all is the side agreement to the NAFTA which ironically is the one that Obama was vociferous in criticizing during his Presidential campaign. While it is true that the NAFTA labor side agreement has produced some output, it would go too far to say that it has been successful, even on the very limited ambitions its tri-governmental authors gave it.

The G20 leaders should ... insist that the US government repeal its new barriers to imports of goods, especially from developing countries.

The connection between trade and environment is another issue that may arise in the G20 Summit. If it does, there are several concrete steps that governments can take: First, there should be a commitment to a moratorium on trade or border measures used to level the playing field between countries that have different prices for carbon emissions. For example, the leading industrial countries could pledge a three-year moratorium to allow negotiations to occur within the United Nations Framework Convention on Climate Change (UNFCC) on what border measures are appropriate and when. Second, the G20 could establish benchmarks for progress in the ongoing WTO negotiations on the liberalization of environmental goods and services and on the supervision of fishery subsidies. Third, governments could pledge greater cooperation to address illegal trade that harms the environment, such as trade in chlorofluorocarbons (CFCs) (which contribute both to climate change and to ozone depletion) or endangered species. Fourth, the G20 countries could ask the United States to stop blocking an invitation to the Secretariat of the UN Convention on Biological Diversity (CBD) for observer status at the WTO's Council for Trade-related Intellectual Property Rights (TRIPS). The G20 countries could also support observer status for the International Union for Conservation of Nature (IUCN), an important international organization with a hybrid membership that includes 87 states. These steps could improve the mutual coherence of the trade and environment regimes and provide for more transparency in the WTO's work.

Taking a Stand Against Protectionism

In summary, because trade is so beneficial, the G20 should take a strong stand against protection and should call on the United States to back away from its recent protectionist tendencies. Amazingly, the US Trade Policy Agenda takes note of the November 2008 G20 commitment to "refrain from raising new barriers to investment or to trade in goods and services" and then goes on to criticize other countries by name (Argentina, Brazil, France, India, and Russia) for having "faltered" in that commitment. Yet the US document omits any mention of recent US protectionism or any self-criticism for the faltering in Washington. Can such omission be anything other than hypocrisy in a President's Trade Agenda that includes among its goals: to "Advance the social accountability and political transparency of trade policy." The G20 leaders should summon the courage to insist that the US government repeal its new barriers to imports of goods, especially from developing countries.

Organizations to Contact

The editors have compiled the following list of organizations concerned with the issues debated in this book. The descriptions are derived from materials provided by the organizations. All have publications or information available for interested readers. The list was compiled on the date of publication of the present volume; names, addresses, and phone numbers may change. Be aware that many organizations take several weeks or longer to respond to inquiries, so allow as much time as possible.

Fair Trade Federation (FTF)
Hecker Center, Suite 107, 3025 Fourth Street NE
Washington, DC   20017-1102
(202) 636-3547 • fax: (202) 636-3549
Web site: www.fairtradefederation.org

The Fair Trade Federation (FTF) is a trade association of North American wholesalers, retailers, and producers committed to fair trade. The group seeks to build a just and sustainable global economic system that promotes the well-being of people and the environment, in order to help alleviate world poverty. FTF publishes a quarterly newsletter, *Networks*; provides information about fair trade certification and principles; and offers a variety of free publications such as *Fair Trade Action Guide* and *Trends Report*.

Fair Trade Institute (FTI)
PO Box 12347, Philadelphia, PA   19119-0347
(917) 464-5558
Web site: www.fairtrade-institute.org

The Fair Trade Institute (FTI) is a virtual institute that collects research and analysis on fair trade issues. FTI hopes to enhance dialogue and learning among academics and activists internationally and contribute to an improved understanding of fair trade and its impact. Recent publications accessible in FTI's library include *The Challenges of Marketing Fair Trade*, *Ethical Products and Consumer Involvement: What's New*, and *Cost of a Cup of Tea: Fair Trade and the British Co-operative Movement, c. 1960–2000*.

Fair Trade Resource Network (FTRN)

PO Box 12347, Philadelphia, PA   19119-0347

(917) 464-5558

Web site: www.fairtraderesource.org

Founded in 1999, the Fair Trade Resource Network (FTRN) seeks to build a more just and sustainable world by gathering, developing, and disseminating educational resources about fair trade. FTRN's Web site has an extensive list of fair trade publications and films for sale. Some recommended titles include *Where to Start—Fair Trade Essentials, A Deeper Understanding of Fair Trade*, and *The Conscious Consumer: Promoting Economic Justice Through Fair Trade*.

Fairtrade Labelling Organizations International (FLO)

Bonner Talweg 177, Bonn   53129

   Germany

+49-228-949230 • fax: +49-228-2421713

e-mail: info@fairtrade.net

Web site: www.fairtrade.net

Fairtrade Labelling Organizations International (FLO) is a nonprofit umbrella association of twenty-three member organizations, traders, and external experts on fair trade. The organization develops fair trade standards and provides support to fair-trade-certified producers by assisting them in gaining and maintaining fair trade certification and capitalizing on market opportunities. FLO publishes a regular newsletter, and its Web site is a good source of information on fair trade, including information sheets, brochures, a blog, and various reference materials.

Oxfam America

226 Causeway Street, 5th Floor, Boston, MA   02114-2206
(617) 482-1211 • fax: (617) 728-2594
e-mail: info@oxfamamerica.org
Web site: www.oxfamamerica.org

Oxfam International is a confederation of thirteen organizations working together and with partners and allies around the world to bring about lasting changes that will end poverty and injustice. Trade is one of the organization's top issues, and its Web site provides information about various fair trade campaigns as well as news and publications on the subject of trade. Examples of recent trade-related news items and publications include *Oxfam Outlines Four Stepping Stones to the G20's 'New World Order'*; *G20 Must Put Fight Against Poverty at the Center of Global Economic Reforms*, and *Extension of Trade Preferences Beneficial for Development.*

TransFair USA

1500 Broadway, Suite 400, Oakland, CA   94612
(510) 663-5260 • fax: (510) 663-5264
e-mail: info@transfairusa.org
Web site: www.transfairusa.org

TransFair USA is a member of Fairtrade Labelling Organizations International (FLO), and the only third-party certifier of fair trade products in the United States. TransFair USA audits transactions between US companies offering Fair Trade Certified products and their international suppliers to guarantee that farmers and producers were paid a fair, above-market price. The group's Web site contains a list of resources, which include answers to questions about fair trade, producer testimonials and profiles, as well as links to other fair trade organizations and a monthly e-newsletter, *The Fair Trade Beat.*

United Students for Fair Trade (USFT)

Web site: www.usft.org

United Students for Fair Trade (USFT) is a national student-led umbrella organization working to promote awareness and increase demand for fair trade on university campuses. USFT advocates for fair trade principles, products, and policies by organizing students, conducting leadership development, and serving as a resource to students seeking advice. USFT sees itself as a comprehensive global justice organization that is working to develop a new generation of fair trade leaders. The USFT Web site offers a photo gallery, a blog for asking questions and making comments, and information about anti-oppression and social justice principles.

World Fair Trade Organization (WFTO)
Prijssestraat 24, Culemborg   4101 CR
   The Netherlands
+31 (0) 345 53 59 14 • fax: +31 (0) 8 47 47 44 01
Web site: www.wfto.com

The WFTO is a global authority on fair trade made up of member organizations that demonstrate a 100-percent-fair-trade commitment and apply its ten principles of fair trade. WFTO members are monitored to ensure use of these principles and are listed in the FT100 index of world-leading fair trade brands, businesses, and organizations. The WFTO Web site provides a wealth of information about the history, standards, and operation of the fair trade market, and also contains publications on fair trade principles, facts and figures, and organizations. Examples of publications listed include *Who Benefits from Sustainable Trade?* and *Making Global Trade Work for People.*

Bibliography

Books

Kyle W. Bell

International Political Economy: Free Trade or Fair Trade? Seattle, WA: Kindle Books, Amazon Digital Service, 2009.

Adrian Cooper

Fair Trade? London: Franklin Watts Ltd, 2008.

Dean Cycon

Javatrekker: Dispatches from the World of Fair Trade Coffee. White River Junction, VT: Chelsea Green, 2007.

Jacqueline Decarlo

Fair Trade: A Beginner's Guide. Oxford, UK: Oneworld Publications, 2007.

Thomas Henry Farr Farrer

Free Trade Versus Fair Trade. Charleston, SC: BiblioBazaar, 2008.

Gavin Fridell

Fair Trade Coffee: The Prospects and Pitfalls of Market-Driven Social Justice. Toronto: University of Toronto Press, 2007.

Daniel Jaffee

Brewing Justice: Fair Trade Coffee, Sustainability, and Survival. Berkeley, CA: University of California Press, 2007.

Miles Litvinoff and John Madeley

50 Reasons to Buy Fair Trade. London: Pluto Press, 2007.

Alex Nicholls and Charlotte Opal	*Fair Trade: Market-Driven Ethical Consumption.* Thousand Oaks, CA: Sage, 2005.
David Ransom	*The No-Nonsense Guide to Fair Trade.* Oxford, UK: New Internationalist, 2006.
Laura Raynolds, Douglas Murray, and John Wilkinson, eds.	*Fair Trade: The Challenges of Transforming Globalization.* New York: Routledge, 2007.
Ruerd Ruben	*The Impact of Fair Trade.* Wageningen, The Netherlands: Wageningen Academic, 2008.
Naunhihal Singh	*Free Trade Versus Fair Trade: A Movement for New Strategy.* New Dehli, India: Anmol, 2005.
Joseph E. Stiglitz and Andrew Charlton	*Fair Trade for All: How Trade Can Promote Development.* Oxford, UK: Oxford University Press, 2006.
Simon Wright and Diane McCrea	*The Handbook of Organic and Fair Trade Food Marketing.* Hoboken, NJ: Wiley-Blackwell, 2007.

Periodicals

Rawi Abdelal and Adam Segal	"Has Globalization Passed Its Peak?" *Foreign Affairs,* January/February 2007. www.foreignaffairs.com/ articles/62273/rawi-abdelal-and-adam-segal/has-globalization-passed-its-peak.

Alison Arnett — "Farmers Tell of Fair Trade Benefits," *Boston Globe*, October 20, 2004. www.boston.com/ae/food/articles/2004/10/20/farmers_tell_of_fair_trade_benefits.

Walden Bello, ed. — "Globalization in Retreat?" *Foreign Policy in Focus*, December 27, 2006. http://www.fpif.org/fpiftxt/3826.

Jagdish Bhagwati — "Obama and Trade: An Alarm Sounds," *Cato Institute*, January 8, 2009. www.freetrade.org/node/924.

Jane Black — "Fair Trade Hits Home," *Washington Post*, July 18, 2007, p. F01. www.washingtonpost.com/wp-dyn/content/article/2007/07/17/AR2007071700313.html.

CBC News — "Fair Trade: An Alternative Economic Model," April 23, 2007. www.cbc.ca/news/background/fair-trade.

Andrew Downie — "Fair Trade in Bloom," *New York Times*, October 2, 2007. www.nytimes.com/2007/10/02/business/worldbusiness/02trade.html?_r=1.

The Economist — "Food Politics," December 7, 2006. www.economist.com/business/displaystory.cfm?story_id=8380592.

Pallavi Gogoi "Is Fair Trade Becoming 'Fair Trade Lite'?" *Business Week*, June 18, 2008. www.businessweek.com/bwdaily/ dnflash/content/jun2008/ db20080617_775861.htm

Johann Hari "Do You Want Free Trade—or Fair Trade That Helps the Poor?" *The Independent*, August 1, 2008. www.independent.co.uk/opinion/ commentators/johann-hari/ johann-hari-do-you-want-free-trade-ndash-or-fair-trade-that-helps-the-poor-882551.html.

Jason Lewis "Fairtrade 'Does More Harm Than Good to Third World Countries,' Says Think Tank," *Daily Mail*, February 23, 2008. www.dailymail.co.uk/news/ article-517823/Fairtrade-does-harm-good-Third-World-countries-says-think-tank.html.

Nadia Mustafa "Fair-Trade Fashion," *Time*, February 27, 2007. www.time.com/time/ magazine/article/0,9171,1594126,00.html.

Jason Nardi "WTO-Special: Free Trade or Fair Trade?" *Inter Press Service*, December 10, 2005. http://ipsnews.net/ news.asp?idnews=31371.

Herbert Oberhaensli "No Fair Trade Without Free Trade," *Wall Street Journal*, November 29, 2004. Reprinted at http://yaleglobal.yale.edu/ display.article?id=4935.

Brendan O'Neill — "How Fair Is Fairtrade?" *BBC News*, March 7, 2007. http://news.bbc.co.uk/2/hi/uk_news/magazine/6426417.stm.

William H. Overholt — "Globalization's Unequal Discontents," *washingtonpost.com*, December 21, 2006. www.washingtonpost.com/wp-dyn/content/article/2006/12/20/AR2006122001307.html.

Reuters — "UN Calls Food Summit in 2009, Hopes for Fair Trade," November 19, 2008. Reprinted at www.sikhnet.com/news/un-calls-food-summit-2009-hopes-fair-trade.

Todd Tucker and Lori Wallach — "Fair Trade Victory," *Foreign Policy in Focus*, November 21, 2008. www.fpif.org/fpiftxt/5692.

Andy Webb — "How Fair Is Fairtrade?" *BBC News*, March 9, 2006. http://news.bbc.co.uk/1/hi/business/4788662.stm.

Steven Weber, Naazneen Barma, Matthew Kroenig, and Ely Ratner — "How Globalization Went Bad," *Foreign Policy*, January/February, 2007.

Index